Managing Hard Times

How Five Colleges Survived the Great Depression

Gene Spears

Puddingstone Press • Lees-McRae College
Banner Elk, North Carolina

Managing Hard Times
How Five Colleges Survived the Great Depression
Copyright © 2009 E. Eugene Spears
All Rights Reserved. Published August 2009

Requests should be directed to: Puddingstone Press, Lees-McRae College, 191 Main Street, Banner Elk, North Carolina 28604.

ISBN-10:   1-931778-04-3
ISBN-13:   978-1-931778-04-6

Printed in the United States of America

Table of Contents

Acknowledgements

Many thanks to the librarians at these colleges who were enthusiastic and cheerful helpers at all times, specifically Faye Williams at Lees-McRae, Pat Hinton at Louisburg, Jan Blodgett at Davidson, Julia Bradford at Wake Forest and Ronnie Faulkner at Campbell. Thanks as well to Sue Spears for editing and manuscript proofing.

Special thanks to Russell Taylor, Director of the Library and Puddingstone Press of Lees-McRae College for the time spent preparing the manuscript and working with the publishing company on the many details to get the book into production.

Photographs used in figures 4, 8, 16 and 22 were provided courtesy of the Campbell University archives; photographs used in figures 3, 9 and 12 were provided courtesy of the Davidson College Archives; photographs used in figures 2, 11, 15, 17, 19, 20 and 23 were provided courtesy of the Lees-McRae College archives; photographs used in figures 1, 6, 7, 18, 21, 24 and 25 were provided courtesy of the Louisburg College archives; photographs used in figures 5, 10, 13 and 14 were provided courtesy of the Wake Forest University archives.

Chapter 1—Introduction

"History doesn't repeat itself; at best it sometimes rhymes." (Attributed to Mark Twain)

Today, we hear a cadence that brings to mind that period in American economic history known as the Great Depression. The years of speculative fever, financial "innovation", conspicuous consumption and a widening disparity in incomes between the wealthy and everyone else comes to an abrupt inflection point. Assets like stocks, homes and businesses lose a large portion of their value. Bankruptcies of families and businesses climb dramatically. Banks struggle, fail or are consumed by others. Jobs disappear and unemployment, even by optimistic government reckoning, moves ever higher. What had been seen as wisdom suddenly is revealed as folly. Yet, as Twain reminds us, events are unlikely to unfold exactly as they did in that earlier era.

Today our banks and savings are insured. Our economy has changed from one based on agricultural and industrial production to one based on service and information. The events of the 1930's are recent enough and studied enough so that the political powers are unlikely to copy the actions of the Hoover administration. Our economic "generals" seem well-prepared and even anxious to fight the last war, but the Law of Unintended Consequences has not been repealed. We are almost certain to face hard times ahead. This is written in the belief that the people and institutions that survived the Great Depression have something to teach us.

Unlike today, the Americans who experienced the Great Depression quickly realized the seriousness of their situation. Although most believed or hoped that the economic conditions would turn around soon, they responded rapidly to the challenges that they faced. As of yet, there is little evidence that we have reached that level of acceptance in this current crisis. A recent survey (early 2009) of workers found that more than half of the respondents said they would quit their current job before accepting a pay cut. Saying and acting are different

1

things, but this attitude is very different from the 1930's. Is this a matter of denial, or will it be one of the ways history will rhyme, but not repeat itself?

Colleges provide us with good models of how institutions respond to serious economic dislocations. First, the colleges in this study are long-lived. All were in operation for some years before the Depression – two of them (Davidson and Wake Forest) were founded a century before – and all survived the Depression and are still graduating students today.

Second, these colleges have fairly good records from the 1920's and 1930's. The academic reverence for the written word means that colleges generally try to preserve their archival material for posterity. Minutes from faculty meetings, board meetings, college publications, and correspondence from the president's offices are often bound and preserved. Businesses have a more practical nature, and I suspect it would be difficult to find equivalent material preserved by the few companies that survived the depression and are still viable today. It also seems unlikely that businesses would be so helpful and accommodating to a researcher as most of these colleges were.

Finally, the financial statements of colleges are generally similar and simple to interpret. College income is derived from students, endowment dividends and interest, and gifts. Ancillary operations, like income from bookstores and laundries, are generally a small part of the budget. College expenses are salaries for faculty, administration and staff, physical plant expenses, interest payment on debt, and costs of running auxiliary operations. Audited reports are produced each year and are easy to compare across institutions.

The colleges that I examined are all private institutions. All were church-related, giving them a sense of mission that helped to maintain their morale and gave them a broad base of public support that they could turn to in time of need. All were relatively small when the Depression began, although most experienced significant growth during that period (one of the survival strategies discussed later). All have maintained at least some archival material from the Depression years, though the amount of material varies considerably among the colleges. If

2

some colleges seem to be discussed more than others, this is due to the difference in archive size and availability, not personal preference.

The Colleges

Louisburg College

Louisburg College, located northeast of Raleigh, had its first incarnation as Franklin Academy in 1787. It entered the Depression years as a women's college with an emphasis on musical education. In 1931, the college became a coeducational, junior college, a role it retains to this day. Current enrollment is around 750

Figure 1: Louisburg College 1930.

students, with an annual operating budget of approximately $11 million and an endowment of the same size. It remains affiliated with the United Methodist Church.

Lees-McRae College

Lees-McRae College, in northwestern North Carolina, began as a normal school in 1900 and was Lees-McRae Institute until 1931, when it became an accredited junior college. It became a baccalaureate-granting college in 1990. Current enrollment is about 850 students, with an annual operating budget of $14 million and an endowment of $22 million. It remains affiliated with the Presbyterian Church.

- Figure 2: Lees-McRae College, 1929.

Davidson College

Figure 3: Davidson College, 1935.

Davidson College, near Charlotte, began as a men's college in 1837. It did not officially become a coeducational college until 1972. Current enrollment is over 1800 students, with an annual operating budget of $72 million and an endowment of over $500 million. This is the largest endowment/expense ratio of

4

these colleges. Davidson also remains affiliated with the Presbyterian Church.

Campbell University

Campbell University, south of Raleigh, began as Buies Creek Academy in 1887. It was accredited as a junior college, Campbell College, in 1926, and became a baccalaureate-granting college in 1961. By 1979 it became Campbell University. Current enrollment is about 5,700, including students in graduate and professional programs. Annual operating budget is over $62 million and total endowment exceeds $115 million. The University remains affiliated with the Baptist Church

Figure 4: Campbell College 1939.

Wake Forest University

Wake Forest University was originally located in the town of Wake Forest, north of Raleigh, but moved to Winston-Salem in 1956 at the behest of the Z. Smith Reynolds Foundation. It was founded in 1834 as the Wake Forest Manual Labor Institute, became a college in 1838, had established a law school and medical school before the 1930's and became a University in 1967. Wake Forest University has a current enrollment of 6,600, an operating budget of $880 million and an endowment of $1.25 billion. Its historic Baptist affiliation was officially severed in 2001 by the Baptist State Convention.

Figure 5: Wake Forest College, early 1900's.

As you will read in the following chapters, the Depression years were formative years for many of these colleges. In some cases, they changed their mission, made conscious decisions to expand, developed innovative programs and curricula and broadened the diversity of their student bodies. The Depression years also shaped the face of higher education on a grander scale. Federal loans for college education began during the Depression, expanding the pool of potential students dramatically. College work-study programs that allowed students to off-set some of the costs of college became the norm; two of these colleges emulated the "Berea Plan," developed by Berea College, a generous work-study program that allowed students to earn the majority of their college expenses through work. Later, federal money became available to support work-study across the nation and federal loans for needy students were funded. The Department of Education had firm ideas about the nature of higher education and some of these colleges listened to what those spokesmen proposed. It is no exaggeration to say that modern, American higher education was forged in the crucible of the Depression. It is probably safe to predict that the developing economic crisis will also alter the shape of higher education.

Finally, while this work focuses on the survival of colleges, the strategies that they employed to survive and prosper are general enough that such strategies should prove useful to other institutions and organizations. The book is not intended to be a historical account; nor is it organized that way. Chapters are based on specific strategies the colleges adopted. Some strategies were widely adopted; others were specific to a single college. Some were probably more effective than others. Still, although not a history of their struggles, the greatest pleasure of researching this field was to read the thoughts and words of the men and women who lived through the Great Depression. Their words are often poignant. I hope they will come alive for you, as well.

Chapter 2—Background

The years preceding the Great Depression were good ones for these colleges. Most entered the late 1920's with lofty goals and an optimistic outlook for the future. Similar to today, these years had been years of relatively high inflation for college costs:

> The General Education Board's study of 257 endowed
> institutions as printed in 'Occasional Papers No. 8'
> shows there was an average increase in tuition from
> 1919-20 to 1926-27 from $105 to $179, or a 70.5%
> increase... (1)

The cause for the increase in tuition was the rapidly escalating costs the colleges faced themselves:

> The mounting cost of the educational process and how
> to meet it has constituted one of the most difficult
> problems of educational work. United States Bureau
> of Education, Bulletin No. 39, 1927, shows that the per
> capita cost of public schools in 1913 was $38.31, while
> in 1926 it was $102.05. This is partly accounted for by
> the diminished purchasing power of the dollar, which
> in 1914 was 100 cents but in 1927 it required $1.76 to
> have the same purchasing value. Better kept buildings
> and grounds, more comfortable accommodations, more
> professors for the same number of students and
> increased salaries all cost money. A study of salary
> increases in 302 endowed colleges of arts, literature
> and science from 1919-20 to 1926-27 made by the
> General Education Board showed there had been an
> average increase of 29.8%. The salary expenditure,
> however, on account of a 55.5% increase in the
> number of teachers, had increased the budget for
> teachers' salaries by 102%. The standard set by the
> Association of American Colleges is one professor for
> every 12 students. In 1920 Davidson had one to every
> 22 ½ students, while this year we have one to every 13
> ½ students.

The increase in fees at Davidson, *the one elastic source of revenue*, has paralleled that of other institutions throughout the country. Steam heat and furnished rooms with janitor services, shower baths with hot and cold water, and other such comforts, which, twenty years ago would have been luxuries on the Davidson campus are as essential now as the radio or automobile back home. (1)

Parents of today's college-bound students might appreciate the results of a comparative study of college tuition costs done in 1928:

A study made of 100 colleges, Davidson included, by the Controller of Wittenberg College and printed in the January, 1928, Bulletin of that institution, "taken as representing a fair cross section of the colleges of the country," shows the following charges for tuition and regular fees:

Less than $150....................................9
From $150 to $200.............................30
From $200 to $250.............................22
From $250 to $300.............................19
From $300 to $400.............................13
From $400 up.....................................7 (1)

Dollar depreciation, shrinking class sizes resulting in the need for a larger faculty, higher salaries and expanded amenities needed to attract students (hot showers, for example) all raised college costs. Yet, families continued paying these rising costs and, as these colleges entered the Depression, they were hard-pressed to house the students they enrolled. "The enrollment of the school has increased steadily every year and has now reached her capacity. New dormitories are needed, especially a dormitory for young men, as accommodations are limited already..." (2) "The passed [sic] eight or ten years have been years of expansion... the student growth has been healthy." (3)

Enrollment data from the 1920's available from Louisburg College are presented in the graph below.

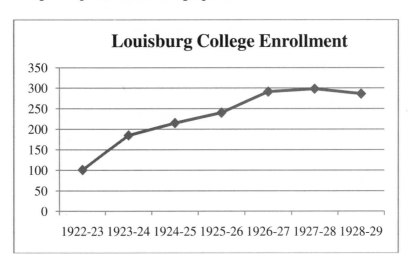

Louisburg College Enrollment

Given these numbers, it is not surprising that several colleges had ambitious plans for expanding their campuses at the end of the 1920's.

From the *Development Program for Louisburg College, Preliminary Campaign Plans – 1928*

Objective: $1,000,000

Payment of bonded, etc., indebtedness	$110,000
Buildings	$490.000
Endowment	$400,000

Time of Campaign:

May, June, July, August – Preliminary work; prospect lists; committees, etc.

Sept., Oct., Nov., and Dec. – Active solicitation. **16 weeks**.

Schedule of Buildings

Building Program:

a.	Chapel and Fine Arts	$120,000
b.	Dormitory	$85,000
c.	Gymnasium	$40,000
d.	Central Heating Plant	$25,000
e.	Dining Hall & Dormitory	$100,000

11

f.	Library and Infirmary	$50,000
g.	Dairy and barns	$10,000
h.	Campus	$10,000
i.	Teacherage & teachers' cottages	$50,000

And from Wake Forest in 1929:

"Concrete Plans Laid for College Future'

To raise $1,000,000 for new buildings and improved physical plant, with which to begin the second century of its existence, Wake Forest will launch a campaign among its alumni and friends as soon as the period of present centennial movement has expired, if the Board of Trustees approves a recommendation of Doctor Gaines. The Executive Committee of the Board has already voted unanimously endorsement of the project. The plan contemplates the raising of the funds as soon as possible, probably in 1930, so that the construction of the buildings may be finished by the opening of 1934. The old college, then, on its hundredth birthday will be garbed in new beauty, equipped with new power... (4)

Both colleges had ambitious goals and ambitious timelines. Louisburg hoped to complete their million dollar campaign within 16 weeks. Wake Forest announced their million dollar plan in August of 1929 and hoped to have the money pledged by 1930.

As will be discussed later, most colleges were forced to scale back or delay their capital campaigns as conditions worsened, though Lees-McRae College still had high hopes as late as 1933:

ASSOCIATION LAUNCHES A GREAT PROGRAM
OF EXPANSION
One Million Dollar Endowment and Half Million
Capital Improvement Fund Sought for College,
Orphanage and Hospital by Trustees

The board of trustees of the Edgar Tufts Memorial Association at their annual meeting in Banner Elk on Thursday, June 8, (1933) voted a million and half dollars' program of expansion 'to more adequately meet the growing opportunities'... a million dollars in endowment and a half million for urgently needed improvements will be sought at once. (5)

Figure 6: Louisburg College students, 1929.

At Louisburg College, the good economic conditions emboldened the trustees to increase the level of indebtedness held by the college. From 1924 quoted in *A History of Louisburg College*:

The college trustees resolved to issue 180 Negotiable Coupon Bonds, aggregating $75,000 and maturing serially 1929 to 1943, and to secure the loan by a deed of trust on the college property. The bonds were issued by the Board of Trustees on March 1, 1924, and on the same day a deed of trust was executed. (6)

And three years later at the annual session of the Methodist Conference in the fall of 1927, the Conference Board of Education recommended "that the Trustees of Louisburg College be given permission to issue $125,000 in bonds for the purpose of funding the existing bonded indebtedness; to pay outstanding building obligations and complete the central heating system." The Board also approved plans for the enlargement and equipment of the college. (6)

13

As we will see later, the high level of debt created great stress for Louisburg College for many years to come.

CONDITIONS CHANGE

Colleges began to notice changes in two important sources of income early in the economic downturn – enrollment and charitable donations.

From Davidson in 1929:

> First, let me say that we have now come to the point
> where we must exercise economy in order to meet our
> annual budget. This we can do unless some
> unforeseen catastrophe confronts us. We, in common
> with a large number of other institutions, have this year
> experienced a slight falling off in numbers of students.
> We could have prevented this had we known six weeks
> earlier that it was likely to occur. It is not thought that
> it is likely to occur again at Davidson next year. This
> has resulted in some loss of revenue we had counted
> on, but we believe that, be exercising the rigid
> economy we have been enforcing, we can close the
> year without a deficit…. (3)

From Louisburg in 1930:

> Reports have it that many of the
> schools and colleges are going to
> suffer decreased enrollment this fall
> on account of the financial
> conditions prevailing. Our
> institution will suffer more than
> some others since a large
> proportion of our students come
> from homes of rather moderate
> means, which are affected more by
> temporary conditions than are the
> more substantial homes. (7)

Figure 7: A.W. Mohn, President of Louisburg College, 1929.

And later that year:

> The present financial cut dealt its blow and with it came the inevitable decrease of students for the institution. Of the entire state, the eastern section, from which Louisburg College receives its major support, is stricken the hardest in this crisis and thereby its support to the college is cut far short. The enrollment of the institution for the present year is only an average of 100 students, the senior class numbering around 26 as compared to the about 100 graduates of last year, and even greater in past years…(8)

From Wake Forest in 1929:

> The enrollment for the first semester was 668. During the semester withdrawals totaled 90, or three more than the number during the same period last year. The number of withdrawals due to financial difficulties was noticeably greater than usual… (9)

Three of the five colleges saw declines in student enrollment between the high point in 1926-27 and the 1929-30 academic years; Louisburg from 298 to 194 (a 45% decline), Wake Forest from 736 to 617 (a 16% decline) and relatively modest decline at Davidson from 642 to 617 (a 4% decline). Campbell and Lees-McRae were just beginning their histories as colleges, and both were in periods of growth in the early 1930's. Louisburg's sudden decline was caused by a fire in December 1928 that caused no fatalities, but resulted in a number of students not returning the following semester.

Enrollment declines were relatively short-lived, or even avoided by aggressive recruitment in the face of the economic downturn. We will cover this in greater detail later.

A longer-lasting effect of the Depression was the decline in annual giving to the colleges.

In 1927, Louisburg College had this to say:

15

Mr. (President) Mohn felt that 1927 was the most satisfactory of his six years at Louisburg College. For the Franklin County Building, $67,914.43 had been collected, and the first floor had been completed and furnished for use. That year he reported that the Franklin County people had paid $67,914.43, with $82,085.57 in unpaid pledges; Mr. R.H. Wright had given a total of $160,000; Mr. B.N. Duke had given $100,000; and the North Carolina Methodist Conference had given $6,955.36, with the amount of $23,044.64 in unpaid pledges. (10)

How different things looked one year later:
> The only income for 1928-29 was $4,791.58 from the Duke Endowment, and $4,020 from the church, making a total of $8,811.58 for the year's income. (11)

This problem was widespread. From Lees-McRae in 1931:
> There is one respect, however, in which the burden is greater than ever before. The administrative board feels that the financial support of the school this year will be a most serious problem. Although Lees-McRae is partially supported by its endowment, its farm and the help of its students, it must still depend on individual gifts. As first one and other regular contributor has decreased his gift or had discontinued to give, the problem of finances has grown greater. Scholarships are needed more than ever before... The budget is not made up of hundreds or thousands but of fives and tens and when those contributions cease some part of the administration must suffer... (12)

From the Treasurer's report at Davidson in 1930:
> There has been a decline in the receipts from church collections during the last three years, as shown by the following comparable figures:

	North Carolina	Georgia	Florida	Totals
1927-28	$6750	$885	$1548	$9183
1928-29	$6552	$996	$1176	$8724
1929-30	$5432	$74	$775	$6282

From Davidson College Treasurers Report April 1930

And from Davidson's President in 1931:

> Perhaps the Trustees have not realized that there has been a considerable shrinkage in the income which can be used for the running expenses of the College within the last three or four years. Until recently we have received $3,000 a year from the Graham Foundation. We cannot hope for any more from that source. Collections received from the churches for current expenses are $5,000 less than they were five years ago. The college is now spending about $7,500 annually on its annuity plan, which was established several years ago. Putting these amounts together, we find that there has been a shrinkage in the income for running expenses of more than $15,000 in the past four or five years. This explains why we let two Associate Professors go, and why we may find it necessary to effect[sic] other economies. If we can keep our student enrollment up to 640 or 650 we will be able to make ends meet without any further reduction in the Faculty... (13)

The annual audited reports give a clear picture of the decline in charitable giving to these colleges, and shows how long it took for giving to recover. Financial data are not complete and different institutions audit gifts somewhat differently, but the pattern within each college is still clear. (No financial data were available from Campbell):

Year	LMC	Davidson	Louisburg	Wake
1928-29	$11,775	$81,631	$6,955	
1929-30	$13,796	$80,726		$4,150
1930-31	$9,677	$82,290		
1931-32		$82,418		
1932-33	$5,062	$79,484	$85	
1933-34	$3,242	$68,935		
1934-35	$2,675	$68,608		$0
1935-36		$70,347		$0
1936-37	$2,916	$82,961		$0
1937-38	$6,829	$123,879	$4,446	$2,900
1938-39	$2,420	$85,548	$5,633	$11,450

Good financial data on endowment performance are available from two of the colleges, Davidson and Lees-McRae, and their income from the endowments generally held up well. Davidson had an endowment of $894,000 in 1928-29, which grew to over $1 million by 1938-39. Lees-McRae had a more modest endowment of $105,000, and ended the Depression with an endowment of $116,000. Endowment investments in these institutions were generally bonds that paid interest income and dividend-paying stocks. The income remains relatively stable over the Depression years.

Year	LMC	Davidson
1928-29	$ 6,429	$ 49,286
1929-30	$ 9,408	$ 49,753
1930-31	$ 7,139	$ 56,086
1931-32		$ 49,700
1932-33	$ 8,381	$ 51,006
1933-34	$ 8,714	$ 47,811
1934-35	$ 7,670	$ 45,308
1935-36		$ 44,801
1936-37	$ 7,805	$ 42,896
1937-38	$ 7,836	$ 43,056

Financial data from Wake Forest are incomplete, but suggest it may have suffered more of a drought in this income stream.   Wake Forest had the largest endowment at the beginning of the Depression - $2.3 million dollars; data for 1938-39 were not available. Endowment income was $161,000 in 1928-29, but was only $95,000 in 1933-34 (a 41% decline). Endowment income did not reach 1928-29 levels again until 1936-37.

Charitable giving remained difficult throughout most of the depression.   Leslie Campbell documents some of the difficulties Campbell College faced when it tried to initiate new capital campaigns even as late as 1938:

In one respect this administration has apparently failed in one of its major objectives. I refer to our two unsuccessful attempts to launch a general campaign for endowment. Two years ago this fall we ventured to employ Clarence J. Owens, of Washington, D.C. to promote such a campaign, but soon found our hopes misplaced and our efforts doomed to failure. This spring Rev. Hugh S. Wallace, a Baptist preacher from Birmingham, Ala., was secured to renew the appeal, but the attempt was short-lived and equally disappointing. To have made two such blunders in judgment seems almost inexcusable and is a source of genuine embarrassment to me, upon whom full responsibility should rest. Because of the urgency of our need for endowment I earnestly ask your careful consideration to this matter at this meeting and your persistent prayers for early success of our efforts… (14)

PRESIDENT LESLIE HARTWELL CAMPBELL, B.A., M.A.

Figure 8: Leslie Campbell, President of Campbell College, 1939.

To summarize, the Great Depression quickly affected these colleges. Charitable donations, critical to the operating budgets of most, began to decline, and did not recover to pre-Depression levels for many years. Endowment income at best remained stable; at worst, it also declined sharply. Student enrollment threatened to collapse as families began to feel the pinch of the Depression. Under these circumstances, the option to increase tuition, room and board costs, *"the one elastic source of revenue"* that colleges had employed for the last decade, was not an option.

What to do? How to survive the hard times? There was no one answer to these questions, but several strategies were developed, sometimes planned and deliberate, sometimes reactive to external circumstances, that allowed these colleges to come through the Great Depression and remain viable to the present day.

Citations

1. *Davidson College Bulletin* – February 15th 1929
2. Lees-McRae College – *The Pinnacles*, June/July, 1930
3. Davidson, President's Report to BOT, W. Lingle, 20th February 1929.
4. *Wake Forest College Alumni News* – Vol. 1, #5, August, 1929
5. Lees-McRae College – *The Pinnacles*, June, 1933
6. *A History of Louisburg College* – 1787-1958", Miriam Russell, 1959 Thesis # 58028 Appalachian State University. p. 87 – 93.
7. President's Report to Board of Trustees of Louisburg College, C.C. Alexander, September 1930
8. "Old College is Facing Crisis" – *Franklin Times* 14th December, 1930
9. *Wake Forest Bulletin* – Registrar's Report to the President, 1929.
10. *A History of Louisburg College* – 1787-1958", Miriam Russell, 1959 Thesis # 58028 Appalachian State University. p. 94.

11. Lees-McRae College – *The Pinnacles*, September, 1931
12. Davidson College Treasurer's Report, F.L. Jackson, 30th April 1930
13. Davidson, President's Report to BOT, W. Lingle, 18th February 1931.
14. Campbell College President's report to Board of Trustees, L. Campbell, June, 1938.

Chapter 3—Delay Capital Spending

The choice to delay capital spending in response to the Great Depression was largely forced upon these colleges, although it could be argued that colleges could have continued building had they been willing to go into greater debt. None were willing or able to do so (discussed later).

Davidson College's president took a cautious attitude toward any new construction when the first hints of trouble appeared. In 1929, President Martin told the Board of Trustees:

> I wish to say emphatically that no further considerable increased expenditure for current or permanent purposes should be made until sufficient additional income to meet the demand shall have been secured. No additional buildings should be added unless additional endowment is secured to properly maintain and meet the charges arising from the activities of each building. It is now rather the accepted procedure to add to the endowment a sum equal to the cost and equipment of each building. This does not apply to income producing buildings such as dormitories. (1)

This did not, however, inhibit the new president, Walter Lingle, from instituting an ambitious centennial campaign two years later:

> Davidson will celebrate its Centennial during the session 1936-37, and Dr. Walter L. Lingle, president of the college, with the full approval of his advisors in the faculty and the Executive Committee of the trustees, presented to the trustees an outline of an

Figure 9: Walter Lingle, Davidson President 1929-1941.

expansion program, both as to buildings, endowment and curriculum, as a goal toward which to work during the next five years...

The general feeling in reference to obtaining this large sum of money in five years' time is that it will be done in a quiet way, and that there will be no great campaign such as has been used in past years.

To familiarize the Davidson alumni and friends of the college with the goal in view, Dr. Lingle's definite recommendations to the trustees taken from the *Davidson College Bulletin*, June 15, 1931 are given below

Buildings

A new Infirmary	$40,000
A new Library	$200,000
A new Dormitory to replace wooden barracks	$80,000
A new Dormitory to replace Rumple	$80,000
A field House for Physical Education	$80,000
A Social and Religious Center	$70,000
An Enlarged Chemical Laboratory	$30,000
Roads, Walks and Septic Sewerage Tank	$40,000
New Church	<u>$250,000</u>
Total for Buildings	$870,000

Endowment

For Library	$300,000
For Scholarships	$100,000
For Up-Keep of New Buildings	$100,000
For General Endowment	<u>$1,000,000</u>
Total for Endowment	$1,500,000
Total for Buildings and Endowment	$2,370,000

The centennial plan called for raising almost a million dollars for new buildings and a million and half for endowment.

It is instructive the follow the fate of the centennial campaign through the Depression years. Here's what President Lingle reported to the BOT in 1934:

24

On June 2, 1931 the Trustees adopted a tentative program in reference to the Centennial of the opening of the College which we hope to celebrate in the spring of 1937. When that program was adopted we had high hopes that much might have been done toward its realization by this time. But we did not then dream of the severity of the financial depression through which the country and the world were to pass. But times are looking better now and the Centennial is drawing near. So it has seemed wise to the Administrative Staff of the College to revive and, perhaps, readjust our Centennial program. We have given serious thought to the matter and are presenting as a tentative program an itemized list of the equipment and endowment that should be added to equip a college of the size and ideals of Davidson in such as way as to enable it to do its best possible work. It may not be possible to secure all that we mention within the next three years, and yet it seems to us that we should at least strive towards the ideal. (3)

In a very short time a very different and more somber tone emerged. A few months later, the centennial goals were even more modest:

We began to talk about our Centennial Program and Centennial Fund several years ago. At that time we did not dream that the depression would last so long and had hoped to be well along the way in the raising of fund for the Centennial Program by this time. The Centennial Celebration is just two and half years off. We are eager to realize within these two and a half years some of the ideals that we have for the College. As yet, we have not undertaken to raise any money for the realization of this Program. The times have not seemed propitious. However, we have been trying to make some contracts and lay some foundations. Perhaps the members of this Committee who are in immediate touch with the business world could advise us as to whether it is wise to proceed at this time in a quiet way to approach persons of large means to solicit funds for the realization of this Centennial Building and Endowment Program, or whether it is better to tarry a little longer. We do not want to be asleep at the switch if the time is opportune. On the other hand, we do not wish to annoy people who might do large things for the College by approaching them before the time is ripe. At any rate, we want the Executive Committee to know that this is a matter that is continually on our hearts and minds. (4)

A year later, 1935, still very little progress for President Lingle to report:

We are still hoping that we can do something for the more adequate equipment of the College in connection with the celebration of our Centennial in 1937. But the general financial outlook of the country has not been very encouraging up to this time. However, we have not been entirely idle. We have been in conference with the General Education Board of New York since last spring, hoping that they might be able to give us a good start on our financial program. Recently the President of the Board, Mr. Trevor Arnett, and one of the secretaries, Mr. Jackson Davis, have, at our invitation, paid us a visit. During the visit we had a long conference with them. They stated that the General Education Board had discontinued the work of helping colleges with buildings and endowments and had turned to other fields of endeavor. Not only so, but the income of the Board has been greatly reduced. So we did not get much encouragement from that source. It is our purpose to approach other educational foundations. I may say that we have also laid our Centennial Program and our financial needs before one or two persons of large means with the hope that this presentation may bear fruit later. (5)

The campaign did not really get underway until the actual year of the centennial, 1937, when economic conditions had begun to improve:

"How is the Centennial Movement coming along?" That question always causes us to prick up our ears and take notice, for we are deeply interested in the Centennial Movement..... It is not an intensive campaign with quotas and time limits, but a quiet movement which began two years ago and is still going quietly forward. Since May 1, 1937 a total of about $80,000 has been contributed or subscribed to this fund. Included in that is one large gift of $25,000 for the new Infirmary which is now in process of erection. From May 1, 1936 to May 1, 1937 about $85,000 was contributed or subscribed to special objects. That makes a total of about $165,000 contributed or subscribed to the Centennial Fund since May 1, 1936... (6)

By 1938, a modest beginning on new construction had been made:

Frankly, the results of the Centennial Movement have not been as large as I had hoped for several years ago. There have not been as many contributions of a larger nature as we had hoped. Our friends tell us that business conditions and world conditions have been uncertain and that taxes have been very high; and we can understand that.

However, there has been much to encourage us. A new Infirmary, of which we are justly proud, has been erected. It meets a most acute need. A chair has been endowed for $50,000 of which $30,000 has been paid in. A $10,000 student loan fund has been created. In addition to these items, something over $245,000 has been subscribed to the Centennial Fund to be paid over a period of two and three years. The collections on these subscriptions will be necessarily slow... (7)

Wake Forest also turned one hundred during the Depression, and started with ambitious plans for capital expansion in 1929, as was noted in the last chapter. By 1930, the plans had become more modest:

President Gaines announces plans of Wake Forest to Enlarge Equipment, Expenses will be kept at a minimum, in order that every dollar subscribed will be invested in a Building.

To meet the urgent need of Wake Forest for better physical equipment, the Baptist State Convention officially approved a plan initiated by the alumni and endorsed by the Trustees whereby the College will seek during 1930 to raise among its own alumni the sum of $250,000 to be used for new buildings....The committee on arrangements decided immediately that the sum which is sought should be used for the construction of a gymnasium and a students'-activities building....The necessity for these two additions to the plant of the College is beyond any question. The present gymnasium is not only inadequate for purposes of general physical education but has been condemned by the authorities of the State as a place for public gatherings.... (8)

Although Wake Forest was able to continue building throughout the Depression years, thanks to a bequest that allowed them to begin the William Johnson Memorial Medical Building in 1933, the ambitious plans for a new gymnasium and student center had to be delayed:

There has been some uncertainty among the Alumni regarding the Loyalty Building Fund money. Some wonder why the new gymnasium has not been built, where the money is etc. It is only natural that you should want to know about this fund since a large number of you have paid your pledges...

Not one cent of this money has been lost. It is true that this fund was on deposit in the Commercial National Bank of Raleigh when it failed. However, the money was not lost, nor any part of it, because the college owed the Commercial Bank a note, which was offset by the Loyalty building Fund account. Therefore the Loyalty Building Fund is intact.

There has not been enough money paid into the fund to build a gymnasium; however, money is coming in daily and, provided the pledges are all paid, it is only a matter of time until enough money will be paid to erect the building. **Due to the general condition of things throughout the country some have discontinued their pledges while others have postponed payments until they are able to resume them.** Some have discontinued them until the building is actually started, stating that they will pay them at that time. The spirit is good and, with the return of better conditions in the business world, the building will be erected... (9)

The second paragraph tells us something about the conditions the colleges were facing at this time. Stories of bank failures cropped up several times during this research. Reading the paragraph closely also revealed that creative bookkeeping was alive and well in the Depression years.

By 1935, the money had been raised for the gymnasium, and, instead of a new student center, the old gymnasium was converted into the student center:

Dedication ceremonies for new buildings are getting to be quite a common thing at Wake Forest; however, this June there will be unusual interest and happiness in the dedicating of the college's new

Figure 10: Wake Forest Basketball, Gore Gym, late 1930's.

29

physical education building, by far the largest building
to be erected on the campus and ranking in size with
any structure of like nature in the state... (10)
With the completion of the new gym, the old building
used for physical education will be turned over to
laborers for remodeling into modern up to date student
activity building. There has been a great deal of
interest in this building from the student's side, and at
this time plans are about complete which will give
them just what they have been hoping for for a long
time. (11)

Lees-McRae College grew dramatically in 1927 when it
accepted male students from the Plumtree Academy, a nearby
institution destroyed by fire that year:

Additional dormitories for boys are badly needed and must
be erected without further delay if the work of the college is
to be carried forward in the most effective way... (12)

Unfortunately, in the recurring theme we have seen, funds
were hard to come by:

Four years ago it was our hope that a permanent
dormitory for boys could soon be erected. Some effort
has been made towards securing the necessary
funds...and some funds have been raised. This is not
sufficient, however, to justify our starting work. We
cannot help but feel the time of business depression
will surely be over soon and those....will help make it
possible to erect a stone dormitory for boys. The cost
of the unit will be $45,000. (13)

Still no progress by 1936:

Figure 11: Outdoor exercise class at Lees-McRae, 1932

By 1938, some smaller cottages had been constructed to house the expanding student population, but the continued growth meant continued pressure to build:

Every available dormitory room is filled to capacity. The new cottages made it possible to accommodate a larger number of boys than usual. At the request of some of the students themselves, the old frame building known as the "barn", is being used one

Figure 12: 3-tier bunk beds in Davidson dormitory

more season.

Several boys are housed in the gymnasium. The girls' dormitory is crowded, and it is hoped that in another year we will be able to add enough boys' cottages to permit the Virginia Building, "borrowed" from the girls some years ago, to be returned to them. It is now filled with boys. (15)

The inability to expand facilities during the Depression years also led to housing problems at Davidson (1936):
An important job each year is that of rooming the students. A tedious and difficult one at best, it was complicated this year by having more students enrolled for rooms than we had places to put them....this, notwithstanding the fact that fewer students were matriculated than last year. We have now 12 in the gymnasium, 16 in a residence, 8 upstairs in the old YMCA building and 10 at the hotel. This is additional emphasis that a new dormitory is urgently needed. (16)

Louisburg (1939):
...In order to take care of the unprecedented number of students, we have put three in rooms intended for only two and have rented all available rooms in the local homes. The class rooms have likewise been overtaxed. I regard that this situation calls for a limitation upon enrollment. The crowded condition in rooms and classes hampers discipline and instruction. My suggestion is that the number be limited to 400. (17)

And Campbell (1938), as their enrollment grew (next chapter):
The completion of the other two sections of our new girls' dormitory and the erection of an up-to-date dormitory for boys would greatly improve our accommodations and add materially to our current income. Our present enrollment cannot be greatly increased without additional dormitories. (18)

Private colleges largely depend on charitable donations to fund new building and capital improvements. When giving dropped early in the Depression, capital projects slowed dramatically. Wake Forest was justifiably proud to say in 1936, "...Since Dr. Thurman D. Kitchin became president in 1930 not a month has passed during which some building project was not under way..." (19), but even they had to delay major construction on the gymnasium and student center for years.

Delaying capital projects caused hardship at some of these colleges, as growing student populations were squeezed into old and inadequate living quarters. However, the money simply was not there to begin construction. There is very little evidence that any of the colleges considered borrowing money to finance new construction. As we will see later, several colleges had a strong aversion to debt of any kind, or were already in debt to the extent that additional borrowing was not feasible.

Citations

1. Davidson College President's Report to BOT, W.J. Martin, 20th February 1929.
2. *Davidson College Bulletin* – June 15th 1931.
3. Davidson College President's Report to BOT, W. Lingle, 21st February, 1934, *The Centennial in 1937.*
4. Davidson College President's Report to BOT, W. Lingle, 30th October 1934.
5. Davidson College President's Report to BOT, W. Lingle, 8th November, 1935, *Our Centennial Program.*
6. *Davidson College Bulletin* – September 1937.
7. Davidson College President's Report to BOT, W. Lingle, 11th November, 1938, *The Centennial Fund.*
8. *Wake Forest College Alumni News* – January, 1930, Vol. 2, No. 1.
9. *Wake Forest College Alumni News* – March, 1933, Vol. 5, No. 1, *Loyalty Building Fund.*

10. *Wake Forest College Alumni News* – March, 1935, Vol. 4, No 3, *Dedication of New Gymnasium.*
11. *Wake Forest College Alumni News* – March, 1935, Vol. 4, No 3, *Student Activity Building Assured.*
12. *Lees-McRae College Pinnacles*, January, 1930.
13. *Lees-McRae College Pinnacles*, September, 1930.
14. *Lees-McRae College Pinnacles*, September, 1936.
15. *Lees-McRae College Pinnacles*, October, 1938.
16. Davidson Treasurer's Report, F.L. Jackson, 6th November 1936
17. Louisburg College President's Report to the BOT, W. Patten, May 23, 1939.
18. Campbell College President's report to BOT, L. Campbell, June, 1938.

19. *Wake Forest College Alumni News* – October, 1936, Vol. 6, No. 1

Chapter 4—Expanding the Customer Base

From the inauguration speech of F.P. Gaines, 8th President of Wake Forest College in 1928:

…we may affirm that if, as that great soul dreamed, Wake Forest is to be good, it must in the light of its present resources and opportunities aspire to be a small, cultural, Christian college.
I urge a small college because that condition permits honesty. The basic moral compulsion upon

Figure 1: F.P. Gaines, President Wake Forest College, 1930.

any educational effort is rectitude in the performance of its engagements. In the educational expansion which has taken place within the memory of most of us, the college world, like other sectors of American live, suffered a sort of statistical intoxication. We had no other measure of goodness than bigness. Progress could be stated only in terms of numerical increase. The first citation of merit for any school was upon the basis of enrollment. Resources were strained beyond any pretense of efficiency not only, as we asserted, in anxiety to effect[sic] the greatest good for the greatest number but also because of the power of a fashion, the fashion of magnitude…
This ideal of honesty requires a courage to admit, and a wisdom to define, our limitations. It will strengthen us against the temptation to be impressive by being merely extensive. It will freely concede that **if a college is reasonably well equipped to provide for**

750 students, an enrollment of 1,000 would be more than regrettable; it would be tragic in the indictment necessarily brought against the validity of the work done. Only with a frank acceptance of limits can we hope to realize the professed advantages of the small college; the establishment of uniform instructional merit in every class-room, the fruitful impact of personality, the motivation of friendliest contact. We shall not bow down before the quantitative emphasis. We shall not be goaded into a competitive desperation that seeking projection cheapens our possibilities. We shall dedicate the resources of this college to excellence... (1)

in 1930:
> ...The resignation of President Gaines came as a shock to the College. (2)

A few months later:
> ...It has been suggested that the College should have an enrollment of about one thousand. This number would, without sacrificing personality to the "crowd", largely prevent the existence of a provincial spirit, furnish ample talent for many commendable college activities such as athletic teams, a band, the glee club, an orchestra, debating, etc., relatively reduce the cost of overhead in administration and instruction, and provide training for a reasonably large number of leaders within the ranks of North Carolina Baptists.... Wake Forest would not be exclusive. The College would welcome any worthy student who can meet requirements for admission. The College exists to serve... (3)

The ideals of President Gaines did not survive the exigencies of the Depression. Wake Forest began an aggressive recruitment drive in 1931 and reached the goal of 1000 students by 1935:

Bursar E.B. Earnshaw registered 1005 students for the fall semester, thereby reaching the goal set by President Kitchin when he took over the presidency some four years ago. There were really more than the figure above who wanted to enroll at Wake Forest this year;

Figure 14: T. D. Kitchin, President Wake Forest College, 1934.

however because of the fact that they could not find rooms, some twenty-five prospective students had to leave and go elsewhere… (4)

Except for Davidson, all these colleges experienced significant growth through the Depression years.

	LMC	Davidson	Campbell	Louisburg	Wake Forest
1928-29	204	611	186	286	700
1938-39	260	664	299	403	993
Growth (%)	27.5%	8.7%	60.8%	40.9%	41.9%

In Davidson's case, they were quite deliberate about not growing beyond their physical facilities. In 1934:

The total number of students registered for the present session is 668 as compared with 655 at the same date last year. The present enrollment is the largest in the history of the College. In fact, it is larger than we really wanted it to be. We feel that our limit for the present should be about 650. (5)

And in 1937:
....A total of 669 students were enrolled. That is our full capacity. When we speak of capacity we are not thinking only in terms of dormitory space, but also in terms of our teaching force. We now have an average of about sixteen students for each professor. It is not advisable to go beyond that point. By the first of June this year we had registered our full quota of students. After that date we were compelled to decline a considerable number of desirable applicants.....
We cannot speak for the distant future. One generation cannot and should not tie the hands of another. But we can speak for the present. It is our sincere conviction that we should continue to limit our student body to about 650 for the present. Our slogan should not be be bigger but better. We should not even think about letting the College expand until we are more adequately equipped for our present task... (6)

Other colleges saw increased enrollment as the only reliable source of operating revenue. Again, using financial data from the two institutions with the most complete data sets, Lees-McRae and Davidson, we can compare the trends in college revenue.

Year	LMC Student Fees	LMC Total	Percent
1928-29	$ 9,659	$ 31,304	30.9%
1929-30	$ 10,920	$ 39,824	27.4%
1930-31	$ 16,581	$ 34,195	48.5%
1931-32			
1932-33	$ 29,730	$ 43,481	68.4%
1933-34	$ 35,845	$ 53,906	66.5%
1934-35	$ 26,378	$ 36,723	71.8%
1935-36			
1936-37	$ 25,333	$ 38,049	66.6%
1937-38	$ 33,606	$ 66,454	50.6%
1938-39	$ 43,412	$ 64,632	67.2%

At Lees-McRae, from about 30% of the revenue in 1928-29, student fees expanded to 70% of the entire revenue stream by 1934-35, and still constituted the majority of college revenue by the end of the Depression. In contrast, student fees remained a stable part of Davidson's income through these years:

Year	Davidson Student Fees	Davidson Total	Percent
1928-29	$ 114,223	$ 323,741	35.3%
1929-30	$ 113,445	$ 323,151	35.1%
1930-31	$ 104,491	$ 315,970	33.1%
1931-32	$ 108,410	$ 321,689	33.7%
1932-33	$ 102,659	$ 312,238	32.9%
1933-34	$ 100,259	$ 303,024	33.1%
1934-35	$ 107,531	$ 315,094	34.1%
1935-36	$ 112,020	$ 326,207	34.3%
1936-37	$ 113,773	$ 347,361	32.8%
1937-38	$ 114,438	$ 384,886	29.7%
1938-39	$ 113,302	$ 345,360	32.8%

Less complete data from Wake Forest show an increasing importance in student fees, though not to the extent of Lees-McRae College – student fees made up 22% of revenue in 1928-29, peaking at 40% in 1934-35, and declining to 33% in 1937-38.

Limited financial data from Louisburg College reveals an even heavier dependence on student fees to support the institution – in 1932-33, student fees made up 72% of total revenue; by 1938-39 student fees were even more important, up to 77% of total income.

In general, the smaller colleges relied more heavily on student fees to stay in operation, but even Davidson was concerned about student numbers and worked to maintain their enrollment:

> ...With our dormitory space and the rooms that can be secured around the town, we can take care of 650 students. From a financial point of view, we need 650 students to avoid the danger of incurring an annual deficit in our running expenses. We should not think of taking any more than 650 with the present number of professors and with our present equipment.
> There is a mistaken impression abroad that students pour into Davidson from all quarters and that we are turning away prospective students every year. We are not turning away any students who have the qualifications for entrance. In fact, we have to work right industriously to keep our student enrollment up to the present mark. During the past year we have sent letters to all ministers in our constituency asking them to send us names of prospective students and asking their co-operation in securing these students. Each year we are sending specially prepared bulletins to every high school graduate in a half dozen states. We also do quite a good deal of advertising. Besides the president and other members of the faculty try to make as many contacts as possible with our constituency, and everywhere we go we try to get in a good word for the college. We covet the co-operation of all trustees, alumni, and friends of the college in helping us keep the college filled with students who have good minds, good characters, and high ideals. (7)

Davidson's President Walter Lingle outlined some of the ways private colleges worked to recruit students – using church connections, mass mailings to high school graduates, advertising, using faculty, staff and alumni to recruit student prospects. Recruiting strategies have not really changed greatly since then, except for the addition of permanent staff devoted to full-time recruitment. Such recruiters were known as "road agents" in the 1930's, but were not used by any of these colleges during the Depression years.

Wake Forest developed a recruiting plan to reach their 1,000 student goal that initially relied on alumni and faculty to bring in new men:

Wake Forest College has as one of its greatest objectives a student body of one thousand. The College has practically all the physical equipment necessary to accommodate adequately this number, and it is of vital importance that she be successful in increasing the student body to this number. We have enrolled here this spring approximately six hundred and twenty-five students; we want one thousand. The College, realizing the dire need of an increase of three hundred and seventy-five men, has begun to lay plans to get them. One of the most extensive new student campaigns in the history of the college will be launched this spring and early summer. **The entire faculty is taking part and will visit practically every town in the state, therefore, coming in close contact with the boys who are planning to attend college and visiting a great many alumni.**
Regardless of how hard the entire faculty may work, we cannot do half the real work that the alumni who are scattered over the state, south, and country, as a whole can do if the alumni will lend their support. The influence that you will have over the boys of your community is far greater than that which a faculty member would have; therefore, we are calling upon you all who are out over the country to assist us in this drive. You know what Wake Forest is, you know what she gave you, so all we are asking is that

you get the spirit of the this campaign and cooperate
with us by talking Wake Forest to some of the boys
whom you may have influence with and get them to
come to Wake Forest. You send them to us and we
will promise to make them like Wake Forest. You
liked it, we like, and the boy you send will like it – so
again, we appeal to you as Real Wake Forest men to
get busy right away and begin talking Wake Forest to
some of your best boys... (8)

We have no record of how effective the faculty were as
recruiters (it is hard to imagine that *all* faculty would be well-
suited to the task and few would find it pleasurable), however,
later statements attribute the successful recruiting drive largely
to the alumni:

The fall session of '31-'32 opened on September 14,
breaking all previous records for enrollment. At the
close of the regular registration period over seven
hundred men had successfully passed the Registrar and
Bursar, thereby becoming full-fledged Wake Forest
students.
It will be gratifying to all Wake Forest alumni to know
that during this period the college is able not only to go
forward but to establish this record for enrollment.
The question arises as to the cause of this increase in
enrollment. The answer cannot be exact, as the
increase was caused by several different things.
Certainly one of the causes was that the alumni
scattered all over the country did their share in sending
new men to Wake Forest... The alumni are to be
congratulated and this office takes great pleasure in
doing so... Our goal is one thousand men – a number
we can easily take care of with very little additional
expense. (9)

In 1933:

In the spring there is always a new student campaign
and this year is not going to be an exception. The

42

program for the past two years has resulted in a large increase in enrollment. We have well over 800 students this year, a fine increase, while practically all the other institutions of the State have shown a decrease.

The question has been asked, How do you account for this increase? The answer has been in almost every case, that it was caused by the Alumni becoming interested and urging young high school seniors to come to Wake Forest.

The college is grateful for your cooperation and support. We need your cooperation this spring and urge you to look over the boys in your community as possible students for your Alma Mater. Send in their names to the Alumni office. We will see that they get the necessary material to acquaint themselves with Wake Forest College. Every Alumnus of the college should know at least one or more boys who will be going off to college this year, let us have the boy's name and you use your influence by giving him a few facts about the college. A large number of the alumni do not realize the fine work that can be done for Wake Forest in such a small way and with such a little bit of effort; therefore lend your effort and keep the enrollment up to the high mark which it now enjoys. (10)

And in 1937:

This month about 11,000 young men are graduating from high schools in North Carolina. Several hundred of them doubtless are sons of alumni. One question which confronts them now is the choice of a college… Fifty years ago there were very few colleges in North Carolina. Today there are over thirty, and competition for students naturally is keen. Almost all of the colleges have one or more full-time road men who do nothing but solicit students, but Wake Forest has not found this necessary. Even through the depression

43

years the enrollment has steadily increased, and the quality of the students as well as the number has been most gratifying. The active interest of 20,000 Wake Forest alumni can be far more effective than the artificial stimulus of a salaried field agent... (11)

Another strategy to increase enrollment was pursued by Lees-McRae College. The college motto, then and now, is "In the Mountains, Of the Mountains, For the Mountains", and it reflected the original mission of the college – to serve the students in the mountainous regions of northwestern North Carolina. However, this mission came into conflict with the economic realities of the Depression. From 1931:

...Heretofore, Lees-McRae has been chiefly for the girls and boys of the mountains. It is still for the mountain section, but this year, in view of the economic condition over the country, Lees-McRae has taken more students from other sections than ever before. This was done, first of all, because such a large percent of the applicants from the mountains were unable to pay for their board and tuition. While the school has always given and still gives self-help work to such students, in order to meet expenses it must have a certain percent of students who can pay at least a part of their board and tuition; consequently, this year not all of the

Figure 15: Edgar H. Tufts, President Lees-McRae College, 1938.

applicants from the mountains could be accepted. In the second place, there has never before been as great a number of students forced to seek education at the lowest possible cost. Since the entire expense at Lees-McRae for nine months does not exceed $200.00, many girls and boys from all parts of this and neighboring states, who would otherwise have to discontinue their education, have turned to the opportunities that this school offers.... (12)

We will consider the strategies of keeping your costs low and using work or other goods in lieu of money, mentioned in the above passage, in later chapters.

Louisburg College explored another option to increase enrollment – going co-ed. Neither Davidson nor Wake (men's colleges) felt the need to explore this option. Louisburg had been a women's college for many years, but faced with a severe drop in enrollment due to the bad economy and the damaging fire in 1929 (enrollment dropped from 300 to approximately 100 following the fire), the college needed to expand rapidly. The college addressed some concerns about the move to co-educational in 1931:

Rev. A. D. Wilcox gave the following statement to the TIMES this week, when requested to clear up the confusion existing relative to Louisburg College becoming Co-educational:

Although the trustees have not voted directly on the question of Co-education for the coming year, the plan has developed sufficiently to make clear the following points:

First, that a survey will be made of the number of boys desiring to attend Louisburg College.

Second, that all boys living in Louisburg and nearby points who will not need dormitory accommodation will be received as day students and will be furnished with meals in the dining hall if desired.

Third, if there are not enough boy students to fill a small dormitory such students will be furnished rooms in private homes at the rates published in the catalogue

for dormitory accommodations and their meals will be furnished in the dining hall.
Fourth, girls will be given the preference in dormitory assignments for this year.
Fifth, the dormitory capacity is three hundred. We want three hundred girls to fill that space and we will take care of all the boys who come as above stated.
Sixth, this plan will be recommended to the Board of Trustees for their adoption on May 26th. (13)

The plan was approved by the Board and formally announced in 1933:

After 132 years of service in molding the character and culture of the womanhood of North Carolina, Louisburg College now steps out into the full field of action as a modern, co-educational junior college. Its purpose is to serve the youth of both sexes in such a way as to develop the best elements of Christian character…
The need for schools of this sort is seen with increasing clearness each year. The junior college is now regarded as an absolute necessity by experienced educators through the country. Scores, even hundreds, of junior colleges have been organized during the past few years…. (14)

As noted above, the number of junior colleges expanded rapidly during this time. Louisburg, Lees-McRae and Campbell became accredited 2-year colleges immediately prior to and during the Depression years. Wake Forest, as a baccalaureate, 4-year college recognized the opportunity this represented, and facilitated transfer of coursework from junior colleges to Wake Forest as an important part of the strategy to meet its enrollment goals (1931):

At a meeting of the faculty of Wake Forest College Monday, March 16, a regulation was passed which provides that full credit up to sixty-four hours shall be

46

given for work done at standard junior colleges in so far as their courses conform to ours. For several years junior college students have suffered some inconvenience in getting full credit for certain courses but, now that this barrier has been removed, there will be smoother articulation and Wake Forest will be able to serve her "little brother" institutions more adequately.

Already almost half of the enrollment in the junior and senior classes of Wake Forest College is comprised of transfers from junior colleges…

…Wake Forest welcomes the junior college students. We feel here at Wake Forest, even though the percentage is large, that we are not getting as many students as we should from the junior colleges. We want them to come to Wake Forest to continue their work.

The faculty has removed the last possible barrier, so now we hope that more of the junior college students will make their plans to enter Wake Forest. (15)

By maintaining or in most cases increasing their enrollment, these colleges were able to survive the Depression years. A growing student body reassured the colleges that they served a higher good, that their mission and purpose endured - an unwritten message in many of their external publications for alumni, friends and donors. More practically, if they could increase student income without increasing their expenses proportionately, they could make up for some of the revenue lost from the decline in charitable giving. Recruitment efforts expanded, but the economic depression forced the colleges to utilize another strategy to increase enrollment – they had to reduce the costs of a college education.

Citations

1. *Wake Forest Bulletin* – The Inauguration of Francis Pendleton Gaines as 8th president of WF College – April 25, 1928

2. *Wake Forest College Alumni News* – March, 1930, Vol. 2, No. 3.

3. *Wake Forest College Alumni News* - January, 1931, Vol. 3, No. 3.

4. *Wake Forest College Alumni News* - March, 1935, Vol. 4, No 3, *1000 Student Goal Reached.*

5. Davidson President's Report to BOT, W. Lingle, 8th November, 1934.

6. *Davidson College Bulletin* – September 1937, *Answering Some Questions.*

7. Davidson President's Report to BOT, W. Lingle, 18th February, 1931.

8. *Wake Forest College Alumni News* - April, 1931, Vol.3, No.5, *Increased Enrollment and How it Can Be Obtained.*

9. *Wake Forest College Alumni News* - October, 1931, Vol.4, No.1, *College Opens With Record Enrollment.*

10. *Wake Forest College Alumni News* - March, 1933, Vol. 5, No. 1, *New Student Campaign Begins.*

11. *Wake Forest College Alumni News* - May, 1937, Vol. 6, No. 4, *An Objective For 1937-38.*

12. *Lees-McRae College Pinnacles*, September 1931, *Another Year at Lees-McRae.*

13. *Franklin Times*, 8th May, 1931, *Louisburg College and Co-Education.*

14. *A Brief for the Maintenance of Louisburg College* – 1933.

15. *Wake Forest College Alumni News* - May, 1931, Vol.3, No.6, *Relationship Between Wake Forest and Baptist Junior Colleges Strengthened.*

Chapter 5—Keep Costs Low

As mentioned in the Introduction, the 1920's, similar to today, were a time of rapidly rising college costs – from 1919 to 1926 the average tuition cost increased from $105 to $179, an increase of more than 70% over a seven year period. Let us compare that to what happened during the depression. In 1929, the total costs (tuition, room, board and fees) for two semesters of college (1931 data available for Lees-McRae) were as follows:

	Campbell	Davidson	Lees-McRae	Louisburg	Wake Forest
1929-30 (1931)	$ 223	$ 498	$ (180)	$ 365	$ 215

By 1938-39, total cost of two semesters of college was

	Campbell	Davidson	Lees-McRae	Louisburg	Wake Forest
1938-39	$ 222	$ 505	247	$ 227	$ 215
% Change from 1929	-6%	1%	37%	-38%	0%

Only Lees-McRae had increased their tuition, room and board costs, and this only brought them in line with the others. Louisburg had been a relatively expensive college prior to the depression, but was much more competitive in their costs by 1938. Except for Davidson, by the end of the depression, college fees were notably similar among these private colleges. This suggests that they were paying close attention to the market, and pricing themselves to be competitive with other colleges.

These colleges used their low costs as marketing tools. Lees-McRae in 1931:

> Since our work is accepted at other colleges costing
> two, three, or sometimes four times as much as Lees-
> McRae, we have something new to offer our students,

and each member of the faculty was asked to make a special effort during the summer to induce worthwhile young people from their communities to register here next session. (1)

Wake Forest in 1933:
Every spring there are quite a number of boys in your town faced with the problem of deciding where they want to go to college. This year some of them will not make much of an effort to go, thinking that college is out of question. Wake Forest is meeting this situation by cutting expenses so that the boys can afford to enter college...
This year the President, Bursar and Dean, realizing the trying times, have ordered a drastic cut in all college expenses, therefore boys will find expenses at Wake Forest next year the lowest in twenty years. (2)
(published costs in the WFC catalog do not match this statement – for most students, except for a few reduced priced rooms, costs remained the same throughout the decade – still quite low)

Davidson also felt constrained to keep their fees low, recognizing a potential problem earlier than other colleges (1929):
There is a need for much larger scholarship funds than we have. Some years ago we raised our fees so that the well-to-do student might come more nearly paying what it really costs the college to keep him and teach him. This increase was made with the idea that we would try to provide scholarships for poor boys so that it might be possible for him (sic) to come to Davidson. Our limited number of scholarships and our loan funds are far from being sufficient to take care of the situation. I am impressed, in fact, I am almost overwhelmed, by the fact that there are so many boys at Davidson who are struggling to make ends meet. Sometimes they are compelled to leave college

because we are not able to find any possible way in which they can be financed. (3)

Reducing or freezing student fees was only one strategy to help families afford the cost of college. Davidson allowed payments to be made in installments:

The President's report will tell you of an increase in the student enrollment. This gives promise of a corresponding increase in student fees over our budget estimate. Actual collections, however, are running slightly behind the record of last year because a larger number of students than usual have been given permission to pay their fees in installments. It is my belief, however, that by the end of the year, we shall have no more than the usual amount of uncollected fees. (4)

Davidson's decision to be flexible with their students was dictated by the external events that buffeted the country (1932):

...Since December 28th, however, there have been at least seventy banks to close in the territory from which a large representation of our student body comes. The loss, inconvenience, and excitement caused by these bank failures has made it necessary for us to shift from a cash in advance to an installment payment basis, and in a number of cases, to defer the entire amount of the student charges for thirty, sixty, or even ninety days, until financial affairs at home can be adjusted. **Had we adhered strictly to our printed regulations, a larger number of students would have had to withdraw at the end of the first semester.** This is an experience which we have not had to face before and I cannot predict with any too much confidence how our accounts will stand at the end of the fiscal year. Installment payments scheduled for February 1st have been met, almost without exception, on schedule time. Numbers of other students who thought they would not have the money for sixty or ninety days have already paid their accounts. Our cash collections for the first week after accounts were due on January 6th were $10,000 behind our record of last year. Now, however, we are only $7,000 behind last year's record. (5)

Lees-McRae also felt the impact of closing banks and cash-strapped families on their operating budget (1933):

In view of the fact that the operating income for the remainder of this current school year has been based almost entirely upon anticipated receipts from [1] student fees now due, and [2] miscellaneous gifts from friends, and in view of the fact that the present national banking situation will in all probability restrict individual deposits from which such bills would have been paid, or at least give cause for the individual debtor to give good excuse for not paying his account; and further, that friends of the college who might otherwise have contributed will very probably not be able to do so now for the same reasons, it is imperative that drastic emergency measures be taken at once in order to reduce operating costs for the remainder of this year to the lowest possible minimum consistent with required standards.

In order to accomplish this purpose the following plan has been proposed and approved by an unofficial committee composed of the administrative and book-keeping departments:

1. That a concerted effort be made towards collections of student accounts. (This is about the only source of potential revenue now left open and even this is of doubtful amount.)... (6)

As did Campbell (letter from J.A. Campbell, President, 1933):

…The check which you so kindly sent on D D's account

 first of the week was caught in the bank holiday, and since things are in such an uncertain state, I thought perhaps I should return the check to you and await certain developments. The bank of Harnett refuses to accept any checks for collection or to cash any checks. Perhaps things may clear up in a day or two, or it may be weeks. I am cancelling your receipt for $25.00…. (7)

Figure 16: J.A. Campbell, President Campbell College, 1920's.

Freezing or cutting tuition and fees was not a strategy the colleges embraced willingly. There were some attempts by the colleges to fight the deflationary trend, but they proved unsuccessful. Louisburg College provides a clear example of this. They raised their total fees from $365 in 1929-30 to $425 in 1930-31 and experienced a dramatic decline in enrollment. The data for tuition and fees are incomplete, but the chart below suggests a strong negative correlation between college fees and enrollment at Louisburg College.

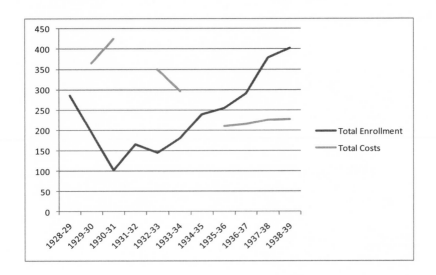

Lees-McRae College developed a more complicated plan to increase the income they received from students. This college developed an early form of "discounting", where the relatively high advertised price would only be paid by students who did not work for the college. Working students could substantially reduce the actual cash they paid, depending on the amount of work they did over the course of the school year.

The need for students who paid in cash crops up early in the depression. From 1931:

> In response to a request to say something about plans
> for next session, Mr. Tufts made some pertinent
> remarks. He said that in order to bring back our school
> to normalcy we must have a certain number of students
> who will pay the new rates or at least the greater
> portion, that at least 50% of the finances should come
> from fees paid…. (8)

And in 1933:

> Mr. Tufts said it was decided in the office to ask the
> teachers if they would be interested in trying to add to
> the enrollment of pay students for next session, hoping
> that indications would be favorable that a large percent

of the student body must pay in full rather than depend entirely on self-help work. (9)

Finally, the college approved a plan to raise tuition, room and board costs dramatically.

From Board of Trustee minutes in March, 1934:
Motion duly seconded and passed that the President be granted the privilege of raising the student expenses for Lees-McRae College to $487 per year. This is a temporary arrangement. (10)

The college made no attempt to raise fees this dramatically, which would have put their fees on par with Davidson, but the April 1934 college newsletter contained this information:
The total cost of a year at Lees-McRae College, including tuition, board, room, laundry, athletics, medical attention, etc., ranges from $320.00 to $380 a year, depending upon the choice of a room.
Of this sum, each student is required to work out at least $75.00 in one of the work projects mentioned above.
It is possible for an ambitious student to work as much as $204.00 during the regular school term. (11)

This experiment in differential pricing lasted at least one year. The catalog for 1935-36 conveys the same information:
Expenses
The purpose of Lees-McRae College is to educate young people at a moderate cost, part of which they earn themselves through work projects. The college desires to explain fully to its patrons the entire cost for the year. Expenses, as itemized below, cover every fee charged by the college, namely, tuition, board, room, heat, lights, water, laundry, library, medical and athletic, with the exception of the laboratory sciences for which a small additional fee

is charged. (See itemized list of special fees) $320.00...

It is the desire of the college to help each student with his finances as much as possible. With this in view each student is required to enroll for work which he may choose, for a minimum amount of $75.00 for the year. It is possible for an ambitious student to work as much as $204.00 during the regular school term. A limited number of students may secure summer work which will pay them in proportion to their skill and abilities. **Each prospective student, when making application to the college, must outline fully his proposed financial program.** (12)

However, the discounted fee structure did not endure long. By May, 1936, the college had abandoned this plan and advertised a much lower (and probably more realistic) cost to attend Lees-McRae:

The average cost for room, board, tuition and fees, for the first semester is $137.50 due and payable on the opening day of registration. For the second semester, the average cost is $109.50. Books, laboratory fees, and personal effects vary with the individual student's need and course of study. (13)

So, total costs in 1936 were $247 per year and discounting was discontinued.

The college had a credible motive for this pricing experiment – they needed cash and believed that those students who had cash should pay according to their ability, in effect subsidizing the cash-poor students who were willing to work for their education. However, in reality, there were a very limited number of students who were willing to pay the higher rates, and the perception of being a relatively expensive college out-weighed any benefit of the extra income.

Discounting is a wide-spread practice among private colleges today. In fact, professional consulting agencies now provide database models to colleges to calculate the discount rate (institutional scholarships and grants – not funded by outside agencies) for each prospective student. Discounting proponents contend that the practice allows the college to recruit the student population that will best fit the college in terms of interests and academic skills.

Another subtle, but powerful rationale for discounting is that it creates the perception of "value" for your costs. So, if a college advertises an annual cost of $30,000, but the college provides a generous financial aid package, so that the student pays (and borrows) less than $20,000 a year, they will feel they are attending a more elite, more prestigious college than another one that advertised an honest cost of $20,000 and did not discount.

While this psychology may work in times of affluence, its utility during times of economic hardship appears to be limited. Public perception changes. Affordable trumps expensive and prestigious.

Citations

1. Lees-McRae College – Faculty Minutes – May 20th, 1931.
2. *Wake Forest College Alumni News* – May, 1933, Vol. 5, No. 2, *New Students*.
3. Davidson College President's Report to BOT, W. Lingle, Fall 1929.
4. Davidson Treasurer's Report , F.L. Jackson, 29th October 1931.
5. Davidson Treasurer's Report, F.L. Jackson, 17th February 1932.
6. Lees-McRae College – Faculty Minutes – 7th March, 1933, *A Plan for Meeting the Present Financial Crisis*, President E.H. Tufts

7. Letter to Charles B. Howard from Campbell President J.A. Campbell, March 9, 1933.
8. Lees-McRae College – Faculty Minutes – May 20, 1931.
9. Lees-McRae College – Faculty Minutes – May 22, 1933.
10. Edgar Tufts Memorial Association Board of Trustees minutes March 8th 1934.
11. Lees-McRae College – *The Pinnacles*, April, 1934, XXII, # 4, *What Does It Cost?*
12. Lees-McRae College Catalog – 1935-36.
13. Lees-McRae College – *The Pinnacles*, May 1936, XXIV, *Expenses*.

Chapter 6—Barter

This strategy of keeping costs low is closely linked with the strategy of off-setting some of the costs of college by trading income for labor. Bartering was practiced by many small colleges prior to the depression (1929);

> …Therefore, when they make application, if they can
> prove themselves worthy and are willing to work for a
> part of their expenses, we let them come… we have
> faith in our friends, believing that they will help
> provide the necessary scholarships. For the past thirty
> years we have been justified in this belief. (1)

The use of student labor to help pay the expense of going to college was formalized and supported by the federal government by the end of that decade. However, two of the colleges that I examined, Lees-McRae and Campbell, took the concept of bartering for your education much further. The first description of this appears in 1932:

> Fifty percent of the students at Lees-McRae College
> are paying either wholly or in part for their education
> by self-help work, work, or in farm products. A boy
> from Georgia traded for his tuition this year 20 bushels
> of sweet potatoes and 150 gallons of Georgia Cane
> syrup. A girl traded in a two year old mule and a cow
> on her tuition. A boy who had won a fifty dollar
> scholarship traded with a neighboring farm to work on
> shares raising corn, which he then traded for pigs, and
> traded the pigs in on tuition at Lees-McRae. One boy
> who wanted to attend college had his way paid by
> cows. His father had uncollectable bills outstanding.
> Trading with Lees-McRae College, the father took
> cows in settlement of these uncollectable (in currency)
> accounts, and paid his boy's way through college with
> the cows. Many girls put up canned foods themselves,
> pickles, etc. and help pay their winter tuition with
> them. One girl helped pay her way with a flock of
> sheep. Messrs. Silver and Pritchett were laughing over

their latest trade that night. A boy traded them an automobile on his education. They traded the auto for pigs and part of the pigs for cash! What they can't trade they eat. And they say they will allow a boy or girl to trade them anything at its cash market value, so long as the thing is usable in the eating or affairs of the institution or so long as they can renegotiate trades for usable articles or food stuff.

We call that whipping the depression, using the noodle, or who can beat it! If education can't beat depression, then who can? If a Georgia farmer, overstocked on non-demand food stuff can trade these food stuffs to a North Carolina college for his son's education, then more power to the father, the son and Lees-McRae! (2)

And barter was actively solicited as a way of getting a Lees-McRae education:

When the banks closed last month, the Association at once announced a series of weekly "trade days", at which all our debtors, of any department, were invited to come and bring goods to swap with each other or with us. These have been fairly successful, in that we have been able to collect some accounts which otherwise would have been delayed in payment.

To a rather unusual extent, the Association is able to use goods of all kinds; food, clothing, furniture, books, almost anything which the average family can use.

The present moment is a difficult one in which to ask for cash contributions. Could you apply the swap or barter system to your gifts to our work? What do you have, that you could cheerfully part with, and that …Lees-McRae could use? (3)

The bartering program continued through 1935:

The catalog further states that each prospective student, when making application to the college, must outline fully his proposed financial program. The college will accept toward the payment of an account produce or other commodities at the standing wholesale market price. In submitting his proposed financial program, the student should indicate what commodities, if any, he proposes to furnish toward his expenses, the amount of work he wishes to do, and his choice of a job. (4)

Figure 17: Lees-McRae College Exchange Store - bartering commodities for an education.

But is referred to in the past tense by 1936:

…Lees-McRae has often been confronted with many problems to continue its operations. Under the able management of Edgar H. Tufts as its president, Lees-McRae has come through the depression, which has closed many small colleges, without a deficit. **To do this has required all sorts of maneuvers to take advantage of conditions as they arose**.

For a time during the depths of the depression the institution was practically on a barter basis. When money was not to be had any sort of livestock, produce

or other local farm output was accepted from its
students in place of the money they lacked to pay their
board and tuition. Always a self-help school, Lees-
McRae in recent years has carried that phase of its
program further than ever.... (5)

Campbell College used a similar system:
"It was all we could do to hold things together at the
time. We even used the barter system and many
students helped pay for their tuition by bringing us
potatoes, corn and other foods." (Leslie Campbell)...
... a record of produce that a student brought to the
school to be applied on his board bill.
12 lbs. of flour
5 lbs of Irish potatoes
4 lbs. of butter beans
3 lbs. of string beans
3 lbs. of shelled beans
14 ½ lbs of shelled string beans
2 ½ bushels corn mean
5 biddies (hens) weighing 8 lbs (6)

My father attended Mars Hill College from 1934-1936
and his roommate paid for his education there with potatoes, so
the practice may have been relatively wide-spread among small,
rural colleges during this time.

The smaller colleges had always included a certain
amount of "self-help", where work was exchanged for college
fees, but the programs expanded significantly during the
depression. Lees-McRae and Louisburg apparently used Berea
College of Kentucky as a model to expand their self-help or
work-study programs. Berea, founded in the mid-1800's, had
established a formal work requirement for all students in 1906
(7); a program that was pre-adapted for the hard times of the
Great Depression. Edgar Tufts visited Berea in 1933:
Edgar H. Tufts, president of Lees-McRae, has returned
from a week-end visit to Berea College, in Kentucky.

On the invitation of President William J. Hutchins he
attended the Kentucky conference on social welfare, at
the famous mountain industrial college.
Berea, largest and most successful of all such
institutions, has much of interest and value to show all
its visitors, especially those whose work is similar. (8)

Apparently greatly inspired by what he had heard and
seen, Tufts wasted no time in putting it into action.   From
Faculty minutes a few months later:
What we have in mind is that every student in school,
regardless of class or standing, will be expected to put
in a certain number of working hours per week. This
will be worked out on a weekly basis since class
schedules will have to be considered. The number of
hours which has been most approved is twelve hours
per week. The details of how this is to be done are
many. It seems important at this time particularly that
we start a plan of this nature and that we start it soon.
It is the idea further that the student under this
particular plan be allowed to select work partly by their
choice of trade. We hope to make this a work in trades.
The student's schedule will partly determine what trade
he will take up. We shall have compulsory attendance
for such work as well as for classes. (9)

The scope, purpose and ideals of the plan were
explained to the public in greater detail in the same month:
Lees-McRae Turns to Vocational Training: Present
Semester Begins New Work Program
Opportunity Offered for All Students to Take Part;
Policy Is to Combine Liberal Arts Education With
Practical Training
With the second semester of the 1933-34 academic
year, Lees-McRae has begun a new policy of work and
education.
In many ways the new plan looks back towards the
early mission days of the school, when everybody

worked. It looks forward also to the new and better economic order the nation is trying to build.

Under the new plan work in the various vocational aspects of the College is open to all students, a majority of whom have already applied for participation. In recent years it has been necessary to take in a gradually increasing percentage of students who have paid cash for all their expenses.

Beginning with next fall however, Lees-McRae will be entirely a working school.

During the present semester, the adjustment is being made as follows: all students may work at a variety of new projects, receiving compensation in the form of credit either on this or next year's school account...

The students of the chemistry department are already planning the manufacture of several commodities.

The next issue of the *Pinnacles* will contain a catalogue of all the goods manufactured by Lees-McRae. To the traditional buckwheat flour and maple syrup we hope to add dozens of other attractions, each the best of its kind.

Educational Values

Lees-McRae is not planning another "vocational school," as the term is usually understood. The training of students in vocations, and especially the discovery of new vocations adapted to the mountain region, is an essential part of the plan but is not the whole story.

Vocations must be joined with a liberal education sufficient to give the student an understanding of his place in the world and the fullest opportunities of every single craft and occupation. The humanities, the social sciences, the physical sciences and the arts are as important for his development as any trade.

So far as possible, as the plan develops, the rigid lines between class-room study and work will be broken down. Is it possible to use the arts in the design of student-made products? The students will learn enough of the arts to so use them. Is business management required to aid in successful marketing? They can use what economics their instructors can teach them. The chemistry and physics and mathematics of everyday life will be joined with the studies of the laboratory. (10)

Next month, the whirlwind of curricular change saw Lees-McRae students already at work:

164 Working Students are now on the College payroll under the new plan of work and education. Under the direction of adult supervisors and student foremen, they are working on the following projects:

Logging and Milling...10
Supplying Fuel Wood..8
Printing 3
Library work and bookbinding.......................................12
Telephone Exchange 10
Office Work..4
Outside Construction and Repairs..................................20
Electrical and Plumbing Work 7
Student Assistants, Lab and Classrooms........................7
Cooks...11
Dining Room 25
General Merchandising 4
Housekeeping 20
Laundry..22
Cannery and Maple Syrup Boiling.................................3
Woodworking...12
Diversified Farming...4
Wild Game Farming...1
Poultry Farm..2

From Lees-McRae College, *Pinnacles*, Feb/March, 1934, XXII

Students were paid fifteen to thirty-five cents an hour for their labor (considered a good wage for the time and place) and were required to earn seventy-five dollars a year – at least two hundred hours of work a year – and were eligible to earn up to two hundred dollars a year – about six hundred hours of labor, though this did include summer work at the hotel the college maintained. A hard-working student could go to the college for a year and pay as little as $112. (12)

Despite this ambitious beginning, evidence suggests that Lees-McRae scaled back the self-help program drastically within a couple of years. By 1936, the college had this to say about self-help:

There are limited opportunities for a number of students to pay a part of their expenses each year by means of work. Preference is always given to those who have been in the College long enough to establish themselves and to prove by their conduct, scholarship, and faithfulness to duties that they are worthy. Of these work opportunities, the majority are during the summer months. The college operates its dormitories as a summer hotel throughout the vacation months, thereby offering work opportunities to both boys and girls... (13)

Was the plan too ambitious, too difficult to implement and maintain? Or did the need for cash-paying students, and the increasing availability of cash by the mid 1930's cause the college to reduce the self-help opportunities?

Data for Louisburg College are less complete, but a well-developed self-help program appears in the 1936-37 college catalog. Apparently, they were gearing up their self-help program just as Lees-McRae was scaling-back on their plan.

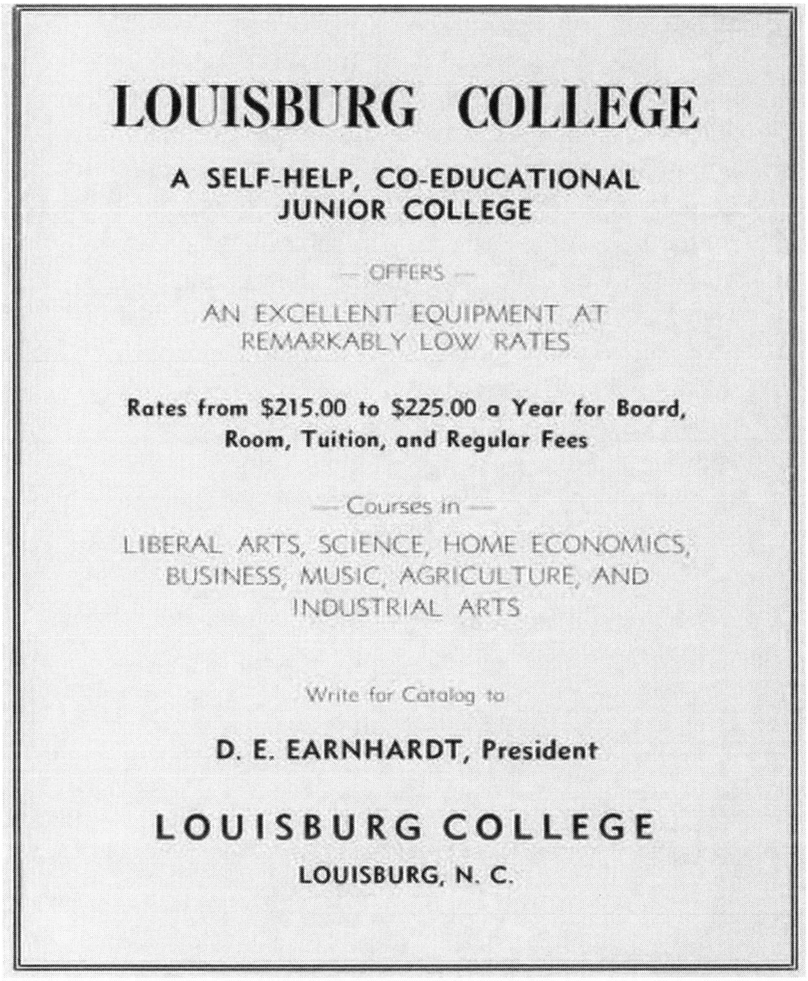

Figure 18: Advertisement for Louisburg College, 1938.

The program does not have the same vocational focus as the Lees-McRae program did, but seems geared more towards reducing the expenses of running the college (much like present day work-study programs). The administrative structure is surprisingly egalitarian:

> Through its self-help plan Louisburg College enables
> young men and women to obtain a college education
> who would otherwise be denied that privilege on
> account of the expense. In general it costs from four
> hundred to eight hundred and more dollars a year to

67

attend any college or university, while at Louisburg College this cash outlay is cut to a minimum of two hundred and ten dollars for a complete college year. In all colleges there are a few students who, by their own initiative, earn a part of their college living; but Louisburg College makes a specialty of helping all her students to earn a large part of their college expenses. In the non-self-help colleges, the work is not systematized and the student makes a little at this job and a little at another job; in Louisburg College the self-help work is systematized and every ounce of labor expended by the student counts and he loses nothing in the process. By the Louisburg plan the student not only receives information and training in the regular curriculum, but he also gets in addition a practical education that comes from active participation in the various kinds of management and manual labor.

How the Self-Help Plan Is Managed
From the incoming junior class of each year there will be chosen a committee of two boys and two girls who will act with a faculty committee of one or more members, one of the faculty committee acting as chairman of the full committee, and this student and faculty committee will decide on what work is to be done. They will study the student lists and appoint each student to his or her work, always keeping in mind what work the student is best fitted and equipped to do. Each job of work will be supervised by some faculty member or student and this supervisor will certify to the bookkeeper of the committee how much work each student does each day. The records are carefully kept and the books will show at any time just what quota of his work the student has done.
Nature of the Work
The work done by the students is not burdensome. It is arranged so that the work will not interfere in any way

whatever with class work and the students' study hours. There is such a variety of work to be done that every student can be accommodated to such work as he is fitted for by previous experience or wishes to fit himself for in the future. It is evident that students will learn to do many things which will be valuable to them in later life.

The young women may do:
Cooking
Serving meals
Housekeeping work in the halls and class rooms.
Office Work
Library work
Day keeping work
Light campus work
Various other kinds of work.

The young men may do:
Gardening
Janitor work.
Landscaping work
Serving meals
Office work
Firing furnace
Heavy kitchen work
Repair work in work shop
Building repair work
Many other outdoor and indoor jobs

How Much Work the Student Does
The usual college year is 235 days including Sundays and excluding holidays. Each student is asked to do one hour of work a day for the college year, or 235 hours work. For convenience of the student and of the college the college year is divided into three parts of 78 days each, and each student is asked to do three hours a day of duty work for this period, or 234 hours

work in all. This means that students are on duty work only one third of the college year, an average of 11 weeks; for two thirds of the college year they have no duty work to do.

What the Students Receive for This Work
It has been figured that $300.00 is the smallest amount of money for which Louisburg College could take any student on the full pay basis. Under the Self-Help Plan the college takes a student for $210.00 for the ordinary literary course of study, or a reduction of $90.00 for the 78 days' work that the student does for the college. That is, the college allows the student $1.15 a day for his three hours work, or 38 1/3 cents an hour. (14)

The self-help program at Louisburg lasted at least through the depression years. In a report to the Board of Trustees in 1939, President Patten states:

Self-Help: All but six of our students this year did work to help pay their expenses. We have encountered no trouble finding profitable work for them to do. This Berea system upon which we operate makes for democracy and industry and economy. It makes Louisburg College distinctive in eastern North Carolina. (15)

There is little mention of self-help programs in depression era material from Davidson or Wake Forest; neither college appears to have needed to adopt this strategy and continued operating largely on a cash-only basis. The only mention of self-help at Davidson appears in 1937 and 1938 information to prospective students, and it mostly focuses on a newly-enacted federal program to help needy students afford college:

Self-Help. During the present session the United States Government, through the National Youth Administration, has been providing work for a large number of students who would not otherwise be able to meet their college expenses. These work positions have enabled students to earn anywhere from ten to fifteen dollars a month, depending upon the kind of work they do and the amount of time they can give. It is not yet known whether the NYA will be continued for the next session, but it is our opinion that it will be. In order to secure an NYA position it is required by the Government that the student and his father shall sign a statement certifying that without this aid the student would not be able to attend college.

Apart from the NYA, a considerable number of students find self-help positions in the boarding houses and round town. The college itself has a limited number of such positions in the library and laboratories. A number of students are also employed in reading papers for professors. These positions are, for the most part, of such a nature that it takes upper classmen to fill them. The College YMCA maintains a Self-Help Bureau and is always glad to assist needy students in securing positions when it is possible. (16)

And so, bartering for labor or commodities was an important strategy for the three smaller colleges. All colleges froze prices, or reduced them during the depression in order to keep and/or grow their enrollment. With reduced giving, endowment income stable at best, and recruiting from a population of cash-strapped families, it was critical that these colleges reduce their expenses. And since the largest expense in most college budgets is personnel.....

Citations

1. Lees-McRae College, *Pinnacles,* December, 1929, XVII, #12, *The Eternal Spirit of Giving.*
2. Lees-McRae College, *Pinnacles,* December, 1932, XX #12, *Whipping the Depression.*
3. Lees-McRae College, *Pinnacles,* April 1933, XXI, #4, *What Do You Have to Trade?*

4. Lees-McRae College, *Pinnacles,* Feb/March, 1935, XXIII #2, *Expenses.*
5. Lees-McRae College, *Pinnacles,* June, 1936, XXIV, *Lees-McRae Ends Successful Year.*
6. *Campbell College: Big Miracle at Little Buies Creek (1887-1974),* J. Winston Pearce, pp. 174-175.
7. http://www.berea.edu/laborprogram/history.asp
8. Lees-McRae College, *Pinnacles,* Sept/Oct, 1933, XXI, *Mr. Tufts at Berea.*
9. Lees-McRae College, Faculty minutes, Jan. 4, 1934.
10. Lees-McRae College, *Pinnacles,* January, 1934, XXII.
11. Lees-McRae College, *Pinnacles,* Feb./March, 1934, XXII.
12. Lees-McRae College, *Pinnacles,* June, 1934, XXII.
13. Lees-McRae College, *Pinnacles,* May 1936, XXIV, *Self-Help.*
14. Louisburg College catalogue, 1936-37, *The Self-Help Plan for 1936-1937.*
15. Louisburg College President's Report to the BOT, Walter Patten May 23, 1939.
16. Davidson College Bulletin – January 1937, *Information for Prospective Students.*

Chapter 7—Squeeze Your Employees

In the Davidson College timeline, published on the web (http://www.davidson.edu/administrative/library/archives/colleg e_history/timeline_CMS.asp) , it has this to say about President Walter Lingle:

> 1929 - The Reverend and Professor Walter Lee Lingle, class of 1892, is appointed President of Davidson College. Despite the Great Depression, the Lingle Administration maintains Davidson's stability and security during this difficult time. The college does not run a deficit the entire time, does not cut salaries, and does not release a single faculty member for financial reasons. (1)

Although not entirely accurate, as these minutes from a 1931 Board of Trustees meeting reveal,

> ...we find that there has been a shrinkage in the income for running expenses of more than $15,000 in the past four or five years. This explains why we let two Associate Professors go, and why we may find it necessary to effect other economies. If we can keep our student enrollment up to 640 or 650 we will be able to make ends meet without any further reduction in the Faculty... (2)

Davidson certainly did the best job of minimizing the effects of the depression on their faculty. The college instituted a hiring freeze, as discussed in the 1935 minutes from a Board of Trustee meeting.

> The Treasurer's report indicates that there is a margin of a little more than $20,000 between our estimated earnings and our estimated expenses. Unless a catastrophe should overtake us I feel sure that all of the $20,000 will not be absorbed by uncollected funds at the end of the year.
> But I hope that you will not get the impression that we have no educational needs. You will recall that we

have not yet filled Capt. N.G. Pritchett's place. Nor have we yet elected a Dean of the Faculty. When we elect men to fill these positions their salaries will cut right considerably into that margin between estimated earnings and estimated expenses. There is also need for one or two additional Professors and Assistants in other departments, but we have not dared suggest getting them as long as the margin between the actual receipts and expenses is so small. (3)

Davidson also abandoned a system of guaranteed rank-based pay raises (the sliding scale) and moved to a merit raise system, where each raise had to be approved by the Board. President Lingle described one of the problems with a merit-pay system, when he proposed returning to the rank-based system toward the end of the depression in 1937:

In 1931 the Trustees adopted a sliding scale of salaries for professors which when into operation that year and continued to operate until the depression made it impossible. In June 1931, the Trustees adopted the report of a special committee which, in part, reads as follows: 'The Committee recommends that in lieu of the present mechanical scale of fixing salaries, the salaries of full professors, as well as of assistant and associate professors and instructors, shall be fixed by the Trustees upon the recommendation of the Executive Committee of the Trustees.'
After working under the present plan for nearly six years, I am convinced that when the budget permits the sliding scale of salaries is better. There are forty men in our Faculty. It is a delicate and difficult matter for the Administration to determine which of these forty deserve an increase of salary in any given year. Not only so, but there is always the possibility of engendering hard feelings. In a small community like this, virtually all salaries are known. In fact, within one hour after the adjournment of the Trustees each year, the most interesting items of business transacted

74

by the Trustees are known on the campus, and in the community. When it was suggested to a member of the Faculty by a visitor that there is very little of interest to see in a small place like Davidson, he replied: 'But think of all the interesting things that you can hear!' Please do not misunderstand. There is very little malicious talk going on around here, but we are all one big family and everybody has a lively interest in what is going on. Now all this may sound irrelevant, but it is not. It has a decided bearing upon the subject under discussion.

On the other hand, a mechanical sliding scale has some disadvantages, just as the matter of seniority in the Army and Congress has disadvantages. A mechanical scale sometimes sends a man up when he does not really deserve it. In a case like that, instead of sending the man up, the College ought to frankly terminate the engagement with him. With that proviso, I believe that the sliding scale is preferable to what I may call the arbitrary method. I am, therefore, recommending in the proper place that we return to the sliding scale that we had prior to 1931, with some slight revisions. (4)

Davidson did economize in staff positions, but again, the economies were relatively modest compared to other colleges:

In making up the budget of expense, every item was reduced to the minimum and we have continued during the year to operate on the most economical basis possible. By purchasing two Dictaphone sets, we have eliminated one stenographer. Several of our employees were laid off during the summer, and we are operating now with two janitors less than we had last year. Our wage bill for the vacation months was nearly $1000 less than it has been for a similar period for the past six or eight years. Many requests for additional equipment and supplies, that in former years would have been approved, have been denied. (5)

In contrast, faculty at the smaller colleges in this study saw their salaries shrink, lost a great deal of job security, and in some cases were paid with IOU's, many of which were left outstanding for years. Staff and administration were also heavily impacted. It is general knowledge that unemployment in the United States rose to as much as 25% during the Great Depression, but widespread salary and wage reductions and significant income declines in many households are less well documented.

Good individual faculty salary data are available from the archives of Louisburg College, and clearly illustrate what happened with faculty salaries during the depression years. These salaries are probably typical of the smaller colleges at this time – contrasting with Davidson where faculty had much higher salaries than Louisburg, and the salaries spanned a much wider range ($2,600-$4,000). (6)

Here are the salaries from all of the Louisburg faculty and their teaching responsibilities in 1929-30. The tables include the estimated value of housing, which Louisburg provided for its faculty prior to and through most of the Great Depression:

Salaries						
Position	Salary	Housing	Total			
Dean & Bible	$ 1,400	$ 105	$ 1,505			
English	$ 1,400	$ 105	$ 1,505			
Mathematics	$ 1,400	$ 105	$ 1,505			
Modern Lang.	$ 1,400	$ 105	$ 1,505			
Music & Voice	$ 1,400	$ 105	$ 1,505			
Art	$ 1,200	$ 105	$ 1,305			
Piano	$ 1,350	$ 105	$ 1,455			
Violin	$ 1,200	$ 105	$ 1,305			
Business	$ 1,300	$ 105	$ 1,405			
Home Economics	$ 1,350	$ 105	$ 1,455			
Education	$ 1,300	$ 105	$ 1,405			
Modern Lang.	$ 1,300	$ 105	$ 1,405			
History	$ 1,300	$ 105	$ 1,405			
Sceince	$ 1,300	$ 105	$ 1,405			
Piano	$ 1,100	$ 105	$ 1,205			
Librarian, Eng.	$ 1,300	$ 105	$ 1,405			
		MEAN=	$ 1,418	Total Faculty=	16	

Here are the Louisburg faculty salary data from 1933-34:

1933-34 Faculty and Salaries		Salary	Housing	Total		
Name	Position	Salary	Housing	Total		
A. Bizzell	Math & Registrar	$ 945	$ 105	$ 1,050		
B. Bray	History	$ 945	$ 105	$ 1,050		
L. Covington	Business	$ 945	$ 105	$ 1,050		
A. Dennison	Home Econ.	$ 945	$ 105	$ 1,050		
F. Egerton	Engineering	$ 1,050	$ -	$ 1,050		
L. Letton	English	$ 945	$ 105	$ 1,050		
L. Stipe	Bible & Dean of Women	$ 945	$ 105	$ 1,050		
A. Gillaspie	Science	$ 945	$ 105	$ 1,050		
J. Vance	Economics & Religion	$ 945	$ 105	$ 1,050		
I. Ziegler	Language	$ 945	$ 105	$ 1,050		
				Average	$ 1,050	Total Faculty = 10

And finally, the salary data from 1938-39:

1938-39 Faculty and Salaries		Salary	Housing	Total		
Name	Position	Salary	Housing	Total		
T. Amick	Math	$ 1,100	$ -	$ 1,100		
J. Cameron	Athletic Director	$ 1,080	$ -	$ 1,080		
E. Craig	Librarian	$ 1,080	$ -	$ 1,080		
M. Finch	Physical Education	$ 945	$ -	$ 945		
M. Kilby	Business Chair & Registrar	$ 1,500	$ -	$ 1,500		
V. Kilby	History & Bldg. & Grounds	$ 1,250	$ -	$ 1,250		
I. Moon	Music Chair & Psychology	$ 1,100	$ -	$ 1,100		
B. Moore	Commercial (Business)	$ 810	$ -	$ 810		
G. Oliver	Science Chair	$ 1,090	$ -	$ 1,090		
J. Patrick	Indust. Arts Chair	$ 1,170	$ -	$ 1,170		
E. Peele	English Chair & Dean of Men	$ 1,390	$ -	$ 1,390		
V. Peyatt	Speech & Dramatic Arts	$ 990	$ -	$ 990		
L. Stipe	Bible & Dean of Women	$ 1,170	$ -	$ 1,170		
Taff	English	$ 900	$ -	$ 900		
K. Uhler	Foreign Language Chair	$ 1,000	$ -	$ 1,000		
				Average	$ 1,105	Total faculty = 15

Between 1929-30 and 1933-34, the average salary dropped from $1418 to $1050 (a 26% decline), and had not returned to anywhere near pre-depression levels by the end of the decade. Salary differential also vanished and was replaced by a minimal "living wage". The size of the faculty dropped by 30% as well, but faculty size rebounded much faster than salaries.

The drop in faculty income is actually much worse that the chart would indicate. The table above includes the **promised salary**, but that amount was not necessarily paid right away. Louisburg was forced to implement an IOU system, whereby some salary was paid in cash, but the balance would be paid later, when the money became available. This is spelled out in a contract letter to a prospective faculty member in 1934 from President A. D. Wilcox:

> … If the tuition income for the current year should be insufficient to pay your full salary this deficiency would eventually be made up and paid out of other income as soon as available. However, you would have to agree that such deficiency would be payable only when funds are available for that purpose. Of course this does not mean that you would not eventually be paid in full as your claim for this balance would be a claim against the assets of the College, and would immediately become due and payable if the College should be closed or go into a process of liquidation… Louisburg College, like practically all similar institutions, has suffered from the effects of the general depression. We are hoping and striving for better days. If you care to accept employment on these terms you may sign this letter which will constitute our agreement. (7)

This could lead to difficult situations when a faculty member left the college:

> It comes to be by rumor without authoritative information that it is likely that you will enter suit against the College for salary arrears. If this is true would you object to giving me that information? I may say here what I said to you in conversation that it is the purpose of the College to pay the salary arrears in monthly installments as we are doing with other teachers who are not now with us. It is my hope and expectation that after the opening of School in September we will be able to pay to you and other

teachers a larger cash amount monthly than we have been able to pay this year. This plan I am quite confident is the plan upon which we have been working and I sincerely hope that you are willing to accept it without resort to the courts.

However, on this matter you are naturally your own judge and will be guided by your own desires. I enclose a recommendation which is very gladly given and I close this with an expression of genuine regret that the close of this year finds us surrounded by circumstances which are painful and embarrassing to both of us. (8)

Faculty at Louisburg continued to accept IOU's until 1936,

...I am very pleased to say that teachers' salaries have been paid in full for the first time in five years. In addition to this we have paid $5413 on salaries due to teachers who are not this year in our employ. That is, we have reduced our debt to teachers in this amount. We plan to continue this method of paying teachers until the salary debt is paid in full, as we hope, without compromise. (9)

And owed faculty salaries were still a budget item at Louisburg College as late as 1939:

Finances for the Year: A study of the Treasurer's records will show that for the last four years our teachers have received their salaries regularly by the month. We are still paying from two to three thousand dollars a year on the salaries that fell in arrears during the depression. We have experienced unusual difficulty in collecting from students this year due to the general business and farm situations back home. (10)

Although archival data from Campbell are less complete, they were apparently forced to the same expediency, as illustrated by this termination letter to a faculty member:

...As I think of your service to the institution this year
I am deeply conscious of some valuable work that you
did, particularly that you did with the young junior
music club. You impressed all of us with your
proficiency in your music training. For all that you did
in promoting better music, I am grateful.
As you know, we did not agree on some matters of
great importance in the life of the institution... These
differences in our training and philosophy of life are so
determinative in our ways of living that I do not
believe we can work together in the most harmonious
way. I therefore feel it a rather painful duty to say that
we feel it advisable to make a change for next year...
As the collections are made on last year's expenses, we
shall set aside your share and send to you periodically.
I wish that we could settle the full salary schedule of
every teacher, but that cannot be. (11)

Lees-McRae offers an interesting contrast to Louisburg
in how faculty reacted to the turbulent times. Generally, faculty
turn-over at small colleges is relatively small, and might be
predicted to be even lower in times of high unemployment,
when jobs were hard to find. However, Louisburg experienced
a dramatic loss of faculty during the early years of the
depression. Of fifteen faculty employed at Louisburg during
the 1929-30 academic year, only three (20%) were remaining
for the 1930-31 year. Of the thirteen faculty employed in 1930-
31, only two (15%) were still employed there in 1933-34. At
Lees-McRae, eight of the seventeen faculty listed in 1929-30
(47%) were still working there in 1934-35.

Perhaps a partial explanation for the different faculty
retention comes from the different attitudes of the
administrations. President Wilcox of Louisburg reported this to
his board in 1933:
...Because the faculty for next year cannot be
guaranteed any definite sum of money, the services
will be like the service of volunteers in any other battle

engagement. **I am therefore not asking anyone to remain and have advised all of them to secure work elsewhere if they can possibly do it. In spite of this, several teachers have expressed a desire to return and take the chances. I also have numerous applications from apparently competent and experienced teachers. From these two groups we will have no difficulty in getting all the help we need without any guarantee in salaries.** But for these reasons I am not ready today to nominate the faculty and will not be ready until perhaps some time in June. (12)

A different tone comes across in the minutes from the Lees-McRae Board of Trustees meeting in 1931:

Motion duly seconded and passed; 'The Board of Trustees of the Edgar Tufts Memorial Association desire to go on record as expressing to the workers... their appreciation of their cooperation in all ways, particularly in the matter of voluntarily accepting a 20% reduction of salary. The Board wishes that it might not have to be as it is but in the light of present conditions we want you to know that this sacrificial contribution is a proof of your loyalty to this Institution. (13)

The loyalty was further tested by even steeper pay cuts. By 1933, further cuts had been enacted, and the employees anticipated more:

It will be recalled that for two successive years all the employees willingly took a ten percent reduction in their salaries. When it seemed that this total reduction of twenty percent would not be sufficient to enable the college to meet its operating expenses, **all of the employees, including faculty and teachers, voluntarily agreed to accept such remuneration as the income of the college might justify and that in the event the minimum salaries agreed upon should**

**not be paid through this method the college should
be relieved from all further obligations and that the
debt would stand discharged**... (14)

Lees-McRae publications were saying:
...All salaries have been lowered by this time to just
above the bare living point. We will compare our
record of economy with that of any institution in the
State, even with the University, which has been cut
more than half. (15)

Apparently, even employees of the state University
system saw their salaries cut, probably more than once. In
1932, the president of UNC-Chapel Hill had written this to J. A.
Campbell:
My dear President Campbell,
I wish to congratulate you, personally, and on behalf of
the University of North Carolina, on your 70th birthday
and the 45th anniversary of the founding of the
Academy which has expanded into the College...
I was scheduled to be out of the State at this time, but
the thirty per cent cut compelled me to give up all
plans and engagements and to work night and day here
in trying to take $270,000 out of our budget in the
middle of the year. We are still wrestling with that
undertaking as a night and day job... (16)

It was not until 1938 that Lees-McRae felt that it could
afford to return faculty and administration salaries to previous
levels:
The Board voted that Mr. Tuft's salary be increased to
$3,600 a year, and that all adjustments of back salary
up to date be turned over to the Executive Committee
with power to act. (17)

It was not only the employees who felt the squeeze.
Presidents and deans also saw significant cuts in their pay and,
in many cases had to take on added responsibilities during the

depression. At Louisburg College and Lees-McRae, most administrators were at least part-time instructors. President salaries were relatively modest at the smaller colleges - approximately three times the salary of a new professor at Louisburg and Lees-McRae (the only colleges with data on this topic).

The small colleges also provided faculty housing to most of their employees; living on campus was, in fact, required of Lees-McRae faculty during this period. Thus, pay cuts were less devastating to the faculty.

Shared hardship between administration and employees, non-salary benefits such as subsidized housing and meal plans, and the maintenance of at least a living wage made the unpleasant strategy of squeezing your employees workable.

Citations

1. http://www.davidson.edu/administrative/library/archives/college_history/timeline_CMS.asp
2. Davidson College President's Report to BOT, Walter Lingle, 18 February, 1931.
3. Davidson College President's Report to BOT, Walter Lingle, 8 November, 1935.
4. Davidson College President's Report to BOT, Walter Lingle, 17 February, 1937.
5. Davidson College Treasurer's Report to BOT, F.L. Jackson, October 1930.
6. Davidson College President's Report to BOT, Walter Lingle, Fall 1929.
7. Letter to Lilly Letton from A.D. Wilcox, President of Louisburg College, June 21, 1934.
8. Letter to Lilly Letton from A.D. Wilcox, President of Louisburg College. May 20, 1935.
9. President's Report to the Board of Trustees of Louisburg College, A. D. Wilcox, May 5, 1936.
10. President's Report to the Board of Trustees of Louisburg College, Walter Patten, May 23, 1939.

11. Letter to Mary Holtzclaw from L. Campbell , President of Campbell College, June 12, 1934
12. Louisburg College President's Report to the BOT, Armour David Wilcox, May 15, 1933.
13. Lees-McRae College, Edgar Tufts Memorial Association BOT minutes, 25th May, 1931.
14. Lees-McRae College, Edgar Tufts Memorial Association BOT minutes, October 20th, 1933.
15. Lees-McRae College, *Pinnacles*, February, 1933.
16. Letter to J.A. Campbell from Frank P. Graham, President UNC-CH, January 14, 1932.
17. Lees-McRae College, Edgar Tufts Memorial Association BOT minutes, 22nd October, 1938.

Chapter 8—Become Self-Sufficient

Becoming self-sufficient appears to have been the strategy pursued by the smaller, more rural colleges especially, and may not have been feasible for Wake Forest or Davidson, both larger and relatively close to urban areas. Lees-McRae attributed its survival through the depression to its ability to adopt this strategy:

> …The Association owns over a thousand acres of property in the Banner Elk region, including farms and self-sustaining industries. These are means by which the three institutions the school, the orphanage and the hospital have kept themselves alive through the last thirty years. On the farms, they have raised most of their own meats and vegetables; supplied their own milk and canned food each fall for the coming winter… (1)

> …The founders of Lees-McRae intended to make the institution as nearly self-supporting as possible. They have a large farm worked by self-help students; in fact, everything is run on the self-help plan. They raised this year 50 tons of cabbage 900 bushels of corn, 160 bushels of rye 200 bushels of oats, 150 bushels of buckwheat, 200 tons of hay and have 5 acres in truck. Mr. C. E. Silver is in of charge of farm, the large flock of egg and meat producing poultry and a dairy herd of about 20 Guernseys. (2)

Farms also helped feed the students and staff at Campbell,

> Accurate records for the past two years show that our school farm has paid good dividends after rental charges have been met. Provisions for a good dairy and stock farm would be a great financial asset. (3)

And at Louisburg College:

> We have had the use of pasture land donated to the College; and we are building a dairy barn in connection with these pasture lands. We hope to have

twelve or fifteen cows by next fall. This will accomplish two things. It will furnish milk for the students and profitable work for the boys. On the land which we already possess, we are building a poultry farm. We plan to have five hundred hens on this farm by next fall. We estimate that five hundred hens will furnish as many eggs as we are now using. We are laying our plans for building a hog pasture and for curing six more brood sows than we now have. These, we estimate, will provide a hundred hogs a year and will furnish all the meat that we need. It is our idea ultimately to run just enough farm to furnish feed for our live stock. We have had the use of twelve acres of farm land donated during the last thirty days. (4)

These farms produced significant amounts of food for the colleges. This report on the Lees-McRae farm (the college was closely associated with an orphanage, which shared in the produce) gives a good idea of the scope of the operation:

Figure 19: Lees-McRae College cow herd, 1935.

The Association farms, including the Elk Valley farms and the farm at Plumtree, have produced the greater part of what the orphanage and college will need this winter. Mr. Silver, manager, gives these figures: 254 bushels of buckwheat (8 acres were planted, a good yield); 145 of oats, 240 of rye, 500 of corn, 200 of tomatoes, 800 of potatoes. About seven acres were planted in a truck patch.

The farms have a herd of 23 Guernseys and a herd of 40 hogs. A registered Poland China boar has been purchased, to start a registered herd. During the summer, the farm kept Pinnacle Inn entirely supplied with country hams and has enough bacon to run Lees-McRae College and Grandfather Orphanage through the coming year. There is a herd of 65 beef cattle, some of them brought in payment of tuition fees.

The farm has raised plenty of feed to take care of its livestock, with 18 tons of soy beans, 75 tons of hay.

The Cannery

The farm produced 1500 bushels of apples, of which one-third have been graded and put in the College cold storage plant, and the others canned and made into applesauce, apple butter and preserves.

The cannery has had one of its most successful seasons, and has produced more foodstuffs than ever before. It would be a most unfortunate mistake, however, for any friend of the … school to consider that they have all the canned stuff they need. It is difficult to form a conception of the quantities used. The school alone uses over 1000 gallons of tomatoes and 800 gallons of peas and corn with other foods in proportion.

The cannery has gone a long way toward filling the larder for the winter, but every can of preserved foods given to… the school will take the place of food which they would have to buy, before the winter is over. (5)

Lees-McRae carried self-sufficiency even further. "We run our own power plant and water system. In short, we have got everything trimmed down to the bare bone of necessity…" (6) The source of electricity for the college was a small

87

hydroelectric plant that the college built just before the depression and continued to operate for many years. In 1932, an engineer at the nearby University of Tennessee calculated how much the hydroelectric plant was saving the college each year:

...Your power load consumption was an average of
1457 KWH per day.
If this record can be taken to represent your normal
load conditions, then under their proposal your
monthly bill would be... $694.60/month.
On the above basis your power would cost you
$8335.20 a year....
Your present power plant has a generating capacity of
220 KW. There are many electrical devices which you
are not yet availing yourselves of, and which, in the
normal course, with your own source of power in
readiness to furnish more than twice your present
power consumption, you will adopt.... (7)

To put the savings ($8,335.20) in perspective, the total expenses of the college for 1931-32 were about $37,000.

The final example of self-sufficiency at Lees-McRae College illustrates a possible risk with becoming overly self-sufficient; you can alienate your neighbors. During the Depression, the college began operating its own "company store", the Exchange. The Exchange was where students made their trades of commodities for tuition or books and supplies, and where faculty and staff could acquire needed goods in exchange for their labor. Local merchants felt the Exchange was taking business from them, and complained to the college. The Board of Trustees formed a committee to look into the matter, who reported these findings in 1933:

We, your committee appointed at a meeting of the
Board of Trustees on June 8th, 1933 to investigate
various complaints that have been made concerning the
operation of the Exchange which was established more
than a year ago, desire to report the following:

…We find that the major portion of the criticism has come from the merchants who are operating more or less in competition with the Exchange… Your committee was impressed with the fact that the merchants here have confronted a very serious condition during the past three or four years. We are of the opinion, however, that the general business conditions may be more largely responsible for their loss of trade than the operation of the Exchange. We explained to the merchants that it was not the purpose of the institution to enter into competition with them, but that it was established to take care of a situation which had grown up here since the beginning of the depression and to enable the institution itself, to assist, as far as possible, the employees including faculty and teachers of the college who have made such substantial sacrifices in order that our work here might go forward. It will be recalled that for two successive years all the employees willingly took a ten percent reduction in their salaries. When it seemed that this total reduction of twenty percent would not be sufficient to enable the college to meet its operating expenses, all of the employees, including faculty and teachers, voluntarily agreed to accept such remuneration as the income of the college might justify and that in the event the minimum salaries agreed upon should not be paid through this method the college should be relieved from all further obligations and that the debt would stand discharged… It is charged that in certain specific instances the rule of selling direct to those not employed by the institution has been violated. It is further charged that in certain instances those who are not so employed have been able to make purchases through the employees of the Institution… Your committee, as a result of its investigation, submits the following findings:

First: That in our judgment some medium of exchange is absolutely necessary to the successful operation of the institution during the period of this national emergency.

Second: That further restrictions should be placed upon its operation and that it should be as far removed as is possible from any competition or interference with the business of the local merchants of Banner Elk.

Third: That if the rule barring sales to outsiders be violated by any employee proper corrective measures be taken to suppress such a practice.

Fourth: That while during the period of this depression it seems necessary to continue the work of the Exchange for the protection of the institution and its employees, we seriously doubt the wisdom of continuance of this business indefinitely, or when the income of the college would warrant its abandonment. We would strongly emphasize the fact that it is not the purpose of this institution to primarily engage in business enterprises, that in its operation no outside interests should be jeopardized and that we recognize the necessity of building up, not only in this community, but elsewhere, a friendly attitude toward the institution which will ensure, as far as possible, complete harmony and cooperation with its efforts. (8)

Growing your own produce and raising your own livestock may not seem especially applicable to colleges or businesses today, but the principle of self-sufficiency can be applied to a variety of situations, and remains just as viable today as it was eighty years ago, as will be discussed in the final chapter.

Citations

1. Lees-McRae College, *Pinnacles,* August 1933 XXI, # 8, *How This Is Possible.*
2. Lees-McRae College, *Pinnacles,* December, 1932, XX #12, *Whipping the Depression.*
3. Campbell College, President's Report to the BOT, L. Campbell, June, 1938.
4. Louisburg College, President's report to BOT, A. D. Wilcox, June 10, 1937.
5. Lees-McRae College, *Pinnacles,* September/October, 1933, *A Good Harvest, A Full Larder.*
6. Lees-McRae College, *Pinnacles,* February, 1933, Editorial.
7. Letter from the University of Tennessee, Dept. of Sanitary Engineering, to Lees-McRae College, December 1st, 1932.
8. Lees-McRae College, Committee Report in the Edgar Tufts Memorial Association Board of Trustees minutes, October 20th, 1933.

Chapter 9—Innovate and Diversify

The financial pressures working on the colleges resulted in a burst of creativity and innovation during the depression. As early as 1931 we find evidence that the colleges were developing distinctive programs to attract new students. From the 1931 Lees-McRae Catalog:

UNIQUE FEATURE—MOUNTAIN FARMING
There is an ever increasing number of high school graduates following the advent of state consolidated schools. With scores of boys and girls—future citizens of the mountains—it is not so much a matter of pursuing further their literary or cultural education as that of making a livelihood. From an educational standpoint our greatest field of future service in the mountains is that which will prepare one for useful and profitable citizenship in the environments of their mountain homes and communities.

There is a real need for adventure along practical lines, to be more specific, there is a need for agriculture. A large percent of the students are going to stay in the mountains, whether they want to or not and a large percent of the mountain boys are going to stay on a mountain farm, whether they want to or not. What are they going to do?

Our answer to the question in the above paragraph is a course at Lees-McRae College in "MOUNTAIN FARMING." The primary purpose of this course is to prepare boys for the business of farming in the Mountains of Western North Carolina. This course can include all phases of live stock and crop production, marketing, farm mechanics, agricultural economics, in fact, any phase of agriculture necessary for the attainment of our objective. The needs, interest, and aptitudes of each individual will be considered and attempts will be made to teach the student rather than the subject.

PROJECT METHOD

Realizing that "experience is the best teacher" the
entire curriculum of Lees-McRae is developed on a
project basis. In this way, theory is put into practice.
The work of each class room department is developed
in the light of some project or problem to be
accomplished. For example, a student studying Home
Economics is given opportunity to put theory into
practice through actual experience in dining-room,
kitchen and practice house. The same is true of
Mountain Farming, Business Administration and
others. In this way, the life of the individual student is
woven into all phases of activities incident to
conducting the College. The completion of an assigned
project is a part of the individual's training. It likewise
becomes a method whereby worthy students may
provide themselves with a means to defray their
college expenses. Project in each course required of all
students. (1)

A new program, geared toward the practical - "it is not
so much a matter of pursuing further their literary or cultural
education as that of making a livelihood" – taught in a new
manner – the "Project Method" that would be hailed as
innovative college teaching today.
Another unique program quickly followed Mountain Farming –
Game Farming.

At Lees-McRae College in March 1931, there was
established a game farm as part of the curriculum of
the institution. The nature of this work is so closely
related to poultry and mountain farming that it is now a
part of the agricultural c o u r s e which is also offered
at Lees-McRae College.

At the game farm the following game bird species have
been propagated: Wild Mallard Ducks, Common
Ringneck Pheasant, Bob White Quail, and last but not
least, we have successfully raised Ruffed Grouse
(native pheasants.)

Game birds can be made a part of the cash income on many farms. "There is an enormous demand for good game bird shooting and even though millions of dollars is spent by sportsmen each year the farmer who holds the key to the upland game bird situation, receives

Figure 20: Game bird pens at Lees-McRae College.

practically none of this money…"

For the young man who wishes to make game breeding his life's vocation and is contemplating taking a course at Lees-McRae College, I will say this: A thorough knowledge of the subjects below will be necessary to fit yourself for this profession should you want to climb to the top of the ladder. The positions that will lead to the top of this ladder will be: Game farm manager for a hunting club, your own farm, the State game farm, State game warden, director of conservation, field work for the State or United States biological survey, game research work, head of United States Senate committee on wild life, etc. To prepare for these positions will require hard work and study.

1. History of game birds and game animals.
2. The relation of forests to game.

95

3. The methods of propagating the various species.
4. Crops and soils as applied to game birds.
5. Scientific incubation and brooding.
6. Knowledge of all equipment and inclosures.
7. Acquaintance with all chart and graph work.
8. Selection of breeding stock.
9. Feeds and feeding applied to stock.
10. Predators and their control.
11. Disease and parasites.
12. Natural science, biology and its seven fields.
13. Game laws and legislation.
14. Business practice. (2)

The new game farm helped the college in another way – it provided an additional source of income for the college. The students learned how to raise and market game birds and sold them to area farmers and hunt clubs.

The Farm has shipped many birds and eggs to different parts of the country during the past season, and, in fact, was not able to fill all the orders which were placed with it. However, after filling all orders, there still remains on hand a family containing 126 pheasants, 127 quail 12 mallard ducks, and 11 grouse. This latter experiment is the first to be conducted anywhere in this part of the country, and is one of the few instances of grouse having been raised to maturity in captivity. The latest addition to the Farm is 35 wild turkeys, and new bark houses have been added also to take care of these new members, together with a new feeding house for the whole Game Farm.

The original purpose of the Game Farm is to re-stock these mountains with game birds that were once here in abundance. A few years will be spent in obtaining a large and select breeding stock before any birds can be released. However, the farmers in this section have already begun to realize the advantages of releasing game birds to repopulate the mountains forests, and it is the purpose of the Game Farm at Banner Elk to aid them through filling their orders for the different species raised here. (3)

Lees-McRae also developed a nursing program in the early 1930's that continued through the depression and developed the first junior college medical secretaries program in the state in 1938:

There is a demand for medical secretaries today. Lees-McRae College and Grace Hospital recognize this need. Students will be accepted in this curriculum after careful consideration. Only a limited number of students will be given the opportunity to enter this field.

Training for medical secretarial work will require more than the usual two years from the junior college. After the student has completed the two-year curriculum, as outlined below, in the college department, she will be expected to spend at least six months, or its equivalent, at Grace Hospital to receive theoretical and practical work under Miss Marybeth Hurst, the registered record librarian.

Graduation does not mean the completion of a designated number of semester hours credit and a designated amount of actual experience at Grace Hospital, but a student is graduated only when she can receive an unconditional recommendation for a position.

In order to receive a recommendation for a position, the student must not only be efficient in her work but also must have a pleasing wholesome personality, which must include a Christian character and appropriate social attitudes.

This is an opportunity for any qualified student who is interested in this new vocational field. No great difficulty is anticipated in placing students in positions after graduation. (4)

Similar signs of curricular innovation appear in the records from

ENGINEERS

Figure 21: Louisburg College Engineer Club, 1933.

Louisburg College,

We have been able also to add another department –
that of Industrial Arts for girls. Mrs. I.D. Moon, our
Home Economics teacher, is taking special training
this summer at Penland to enable her to take oversight
of this Industrial Art work next year. (5)
A new venture of the college is to establish a two-year
Agricultural Terminal Course planned to meet the
needs of the young man who desires to return to the
farm, as a life vocation. Such a course is not now
offered in any of our colleges in Eastern North
Carolina. The demand for such a course by several
students assures us that it will meet a great need. The
instructor for this work has not as yet been employed,
but some efficient men have been recommended. This
course has been planned with the advice of the
Agricultural Authorities of State College and other
experienced leaders. (Other secondary courses have

been adjusted leading to nursing, medicine, dentistry, pharmacy, and medical-secretarial.) (6)

Campbell College,
While it is our conviction that nothing should replace our emphasis upon broad general preparatory education, some vocational training is much needed as

Figure 22: Campbell Commercial Class, 1939.

an accompaniment in many instances. With this conviction we have strengthened the Commercial Department by the addition of a teacher for shorthand and typewriting. A new home economics department, established on the cottage plan for practical training, has been introduced. This year we probably established a precedent among junior colleges by offering for credit a course in playwriting and play production, with gratifying results. (7)

And Wake Forest College,
To meet the needs of a considerable number of its students who desire to become coaches and physical education directors in high schools, Wake Forest will offer next spring, for the first time, a course in Physical Education which will rank with the best.
Instructors in this department will be members of the coaching staff and several of the medical school faculty. The courses will carry degree credit, a maximum of four hours in physical education being allowed on the 124 required for graduation.

99

The department… will offer courses in anatomy, physiology and hygiene, bandaging and massage, first aid, remedial exercises, gymnastics, golf, tennis, football, basketball, and baseball. A course will be given also in administration of recreational programs. (8)

Some of the innovations went beyond new courses as colleges experimented with new degrees and new programs. Lees-McRae experimented with a "graduate" program of vocational training after the student completed the two-year degree, proposed in 1934:

I would like to have your reaction to the proposed Third-Year Plan, and would like for you to keep the following points in mind as follows. I will call upon each faculty member for an opinion within a day or so before faculty meeting:

1. That it can be called vocational year, or post-graduate year, or third-year plan.
2. That it does not affect our position as a junior college.
3. That it is using more definitely the equipment and training which we can give a few students who are wanting that type of work.
4. That it will perform the task of fulfilling one of the objectives of Lees-McRae College - that of vocational training.
5. That I want an interview with each one and get any opinions or suggestions on the plan. I will interview each of you personally before the faculty meeting Tuesday next.
8. That there seems to be a need from students' reports.
7. That it is desired that the faculty approve it in their minutes.
8. That it is then to go before the Board of Trustees for their action.
Sincerely,
Leo K. Pritchett (Dean) (9)

and ready for implementation by the 1935 academic year. The curriculum is included in some detail below to give an idea of the ambitious scope of the new degree.

This year of preparation in selected vocations is primarily for those students of mountain areas who have graduated from the Junior College and who do not wish to continue their education at some traditional senior college but rather to prepare themselves better in some vocation which Lees-McRae offers in this third year.

Under this plan of study a "year" means a project year and not the academic year. You have completed your course when you have satisfactorily completed your project, whether it is six months, nine months, or eighteen months.

You will learn by doing. It is evident that one does not learn to swim by reading how to do it but by actually trying to swim. You will learn poultry by actually working with poultry; learn wood work by working in the wood shop, etc., and you will work and study under the sympathetic supervision of competent instructors... Some of these vocations can be used on the farm as a monetary "crop". As one example, with the mountain areas rapidly developing as resorts, opportunities are coming for shops and inns or tea rooms. This method of education may be what you have been looking for. Think.

CURRICULA IN SELECTED VOCATIONS

CURRICULA IN VOCATIONAL AGRICULTURE

These curricula are for students who are interested in farming in order that they may go back to their farms as better farmers or work for others along lines of agriculture.

FIELDS OF SPECIALIZATION

General Agriculture
If the student wishes to know more about the general
farming, the following subjects will be studied:
Farm Equipment, General Animal Husbandry, General
Field Crops, General Horticulture, General Poultry,
Soil Geology.
Field Crops Cereals, Farm Equipment, Grasses,
Legumes.

CURRICULA IN THE SCIENCE DEPARTMENT
FIELDS OF SPECIALIZATION
Electrical Course
This course should prepare a student as general
electrician, for community distribution systems, for
meter reading or meter testing and keeping meter
records for some Power Company or prepare him for
other related fields such as electrifying of home and
farm in rural community, sale and record keeping of
Power and installation home units etc…

Steam Power Plant
1. Proper firing of boilers. 2. Care of plant machinery.
3. Cost of producing heat delivered to the buildings
complete cost records. 4. Power plant chemistry.
Livestock Farming
Animal Breeding, Animal Nutrition, Beef Cattle
Production, Diseases of Cattle, Diseases of Swine,
Farm Butchering, History of Beef Cattle, Home
Tanning, Judging Beef Cattle, Judging Swine, Swine
Production.
Dairying
Animal Breeding, Animal Nutrition, Dairy Cattle and
Milk Production, Diseases of Cattle, Herd
Improvement, History of Dairy Cattle, Judging Dairy
Cattle.
Horticulture
General Horticulture, Small Fruit Culture, Vegetable
Forcing, Vegetable Production.

Poultry
Incubation and Brooding, Poultry Diseases, Poultry Nutrition.

CURRICULA IN THE WOOD WORK DEPARTMENT
Fields of Specialization
Cabinet Work
This branch will consist of the planning, drafting, and construction of a complete set of furniture suitable for a home or office building. It will involve complete mastery of all machines, tools and operations involved in cabinet work together with an analysis of the work, the exact cost and economic value of the product, the detailed plans, records of information and the finished product will be proof of the completion of the project.
Architecture
This project will include a complete architectural problem from the planning of the landscape through the planning and building of a completed building. The plans to be designed, drawn and blue-printed and executed by or under the supervision of the student, the structure to be modern in design and complete in every detail.
Forestry
This project will include a complete reforestation project with draftings of the area reforested, order of planting, diagrams of trees, their soil requirements, the soil composition of the area, the methods and time of planting, diseases and pests and their treatment. The economic value will be charted to cover the period from planting until harvest. The student will be expected to secure and organize all information and records and furnish them in evidence of the finished project.
Landscape Gardening
This project will consist in the selection, designing, drafting, and execution of a landscape or series of

landscapes. The project selected will be one involving the change of an area which is not pleasing to look upon or economical to maintain in the community in its present condition, to so change it as to make it beautiful and economical for the community. The plans for such a project are to be completed in detail by the student and the actual work required for the execution of the plans will be directly under his supervision. Such information as will be necessary for the project and any help needed by the student to aid him in his plans and his work will be supplied by the instructor in charge.

CURRICULA IN WROUGHT IRON
Fields of Specialization
General Repair Blacksmithing (Including Horse Shoeing)
This course is designed for the students who wish to operate a shop on their farm for the community or to operate a shop in some small community. This course will include all types of repair work in wrought iron such as farm machinery, etc.
Course in Tool Smithing and Steel Sharpening
This course will give a student training in making and repairing tools and the sharpening of steel. Special emphasis will be made in tempering steel. There are but few workers who can take the temper out of steel; fewer still who can put the temper back in steel properly. This is a good field for practical application for any boy whether on farm or in the shop.
Course in Sheet Metal Work
This course will be adapted to the individuals needs in sheet and metal work, drafting, planning and execution of sheet metal jobs will be stressed.
Course in Ornamental Iron Work
This course is not designed to prepare the student to be an expert in ornamental work but to give him the basic fundamentals and the making of a few simple

ornamental pieces. One becomes an expert in this field only by years of study and experience.

Figure 23: Daniel Boone VI, teaching iron work at Lees-McRae College.

CURRICULA IN HOME ECONOMICS
Fields of Specialization
These courses are for girls who do not wish to complete sufficient work for a degree in Home Economics but are interested in vocational training which will either fit them for home making or positions requiring knowledge of some phase of home economics.

Hotel and Tea Room Management

This project is to include a general course in the study of foods, with special emphasis on food value, preparation and serving, and purchasing of foods. The student will be given the opportunity of receiving actual experience on the job under the direction of the college dietitian.

Child Care

This course is designed for students who are interested in kindergarten teaching, for orphanage workers and nursery school workers. The course will be a continuation of the child care course as outlined for the senior girls, with actual experience in caring for children in Grandfather Home under direction of Miss Russell.

Shop Managers

These projects are to be divided into three or more divisions and will include training in operating.

General Home Making Course

This course is designed for girls who are not planning to go on to college or planning to go into any gainful occupation.

These courses will include: 1. Foods. 2. Clothing. 3. Home Manage. 4. Child Care. 5. Family Relation.

CURRICULA IN WEAVING
Fields of Specialization

Weaving for the Gift Shop

This division would include specialized patterns and pieces, special weaves, and the use of specialized looms for quantity production for gift shop sale and as such would be a distinct asset to girls taking the gift shop management courses in the Home Economics division.

Weaving as an Art or for Family Use

For those interested in weaving either as an art course or in connection with home economics, courses may be organized with the object in view of preparing the student in all the phases of weaving design, technical processes, hand dyeing and the finishing of woven fabrics, including the weaving of pieces for the home and of hand loomed clothing fabrics.

THE SCHOOL OF NURSING

The requirements for entrance to schools of nursing are gradually being raised to at least a minimum of one year of college work. Many schools of nursing have already raised their standards to require at least one year of college work, definitely prescribing certain

106

courses. Others are strongly advising the student to take at least two years of college work before enrolling in the School of Nursing. (10)

Wake Forest already had post-graduate programs in medicine and law, but, responding to the economic forces working on their students, they innovated by compressing their curriculum in these programs to cut a year of study from them:

Two important changes have been made relative to requirements for degrees beginning with the year 1935-36. They affect the degrees of Bachelor of Laws and Bachelor of Science.

Beginning next year a student may receive the BA and LLB degrees in six years instead of seven, while the medical degree will be given one year earlier than it has been granted in the past.

The changes relative to the law degree permit a student to take the required academic work in three years, receive the BA degree upon completion of his first year in the law school, and after two more years in law receive the LLB degree.

Students entering the school of medicine after the three year period of academic work, may receive the BS degree at the end of their first year of medical study, taking the second year as post graduate work. The Certificate in Medicine and the degree of Bachelor of Science in Medicine will be discontinued.

These changes are permissive, not compulsory, aiming to encourage students desiring a professional education to work for one of the academic degrees as well. (11)

A recurring theme in these instances of curricular innovation and change is an emphasis on practical education that would improve a student's chances of finding work after college. The colleges were responding to customer demand and larger societal pressures. We get a perspective of the educational milieu within which the colleges were operating in this publication from Lees-McRae College in 1937:

...Today economists tell us that conditions are returning to normal. True as that may be according to statistics and figures, it does not mean that we are returning to pre-depression attitudes towards life. The lessons of depression have left their mark and we are in a new world. Facing educators all over the country is the question of how schools can fit into this new era...

More Practical Education Needed

Another statement from Mr. Lang, who has had opportunities to observe youth problems both in CCC camps and in college, emphasizes the need for more practical education. "Certainly," he says in a recent issue of the New York Times, "we do not wish to base education on a materialistic philosophy, yet youth must be prepared for a world of reality, in which earning a living and adjusting to contemporary conditions are essential." The picture of a young graduate passing from the halls of learning, his hand clasping a diploma, his face lighted with the vision of the future, is no longer a picture that thrills and inspires. It arouses pity and chills the heart, unless we know what the training within those halls has been. No longer is a diploma a passport into success. To be of any value it must represent definite preparation for living. Today the world is demanding more of its young people than ever before. "We must drive home, once and for all, that it is the trained person in any field, the person who can use tools in the vocations or in handicraft who is the best asset of the country..."

Positions More Numerous

Robert F. Moore, secretary of appointments of Columbia University, in his recent annual report to Dr. Nicholas Murray Butler, said that positions for college trained men and women will be more numerous in 1937 than any time since the boom years of the twenties. In urging the need for more practical education Mr. Moore suggested that colleges adopt a system of 'apprenticing' students in offices, stores and industrial occupations during the summer vacations. He also proposed that every student should be asked "to choose a definite future course and call a halt if has been merely pleasantly drifting without purpose through an unspecialized academic curriculum." What part has Lees-McRae in this movement for more practical education? At present, by requiring all students to spend at least two days a week in some practical work, the college is carrying out its objective of teaching by practice and enabling students to learn by actually working at a job. This is really an expansion of the old trades idea which combines with apprenticeship two years of cultural training. Not all of the jobs in which students are engaged can be considered 'apprentice' work, since they do not always lead to definite vocations; yet even the humblest of these jobs give training which should prove valuable to a worker in any field.... (12)

Another practical innovation implemented by Lees-McRae was the creation of an Alumni placement service, to find jobs for students in a time of heavy unemployment, 1933:

Lees-McRae College Opens Alumni Placement Service for Recent Graduates. Friends May Help. The present outlook in the business world is brighter than it has been. It is reasonable to suppose that before very long many idle wheels will be turning again, and a number of people will go back to work. When you find, in your business or even in your home, that you can use additional help, will you think of Banner Elk? We are graduating this spring the largest and best-prepared class of boys and girls the school has yet had, and we are anxious to help as many as possible of them to find work.

Herewith are some of the arts and trades members of
the present graduating class have learned (by hard
work in return for their education):

Three girls are experienced cooks. Nine girls are
trained in housekeeping work, some having had
complete and successful charge of private households;
four girls, as expert waitresses; two, as dishwashers;
and one, as telephone operator. A number are very
well fitted for work as governesses or nurses, in
combination perhaps with this other work.

Among the boys there is even greater variety. Two are
trained bookkeepers; two are skilled assistants on the
College Game Farm, and are qualified to start such an
enterprise elsewhere; one has had months of
experience as lifeguard; three, in library work of all
kinds; two as cooks; one, as a butcher; one as a
manager of a small general store; one, as a laundry
operator; one, in heavy construction work; two, in the
poultry farm business; two, as hotel bell-hops and
porters; one in carpenter and general repair work. (13)

Davidson, who entered the depression in the best financial
shape of these colleges, is an exception to this trend, although
they, too, felt the pressures to change, to move towards a more
practical, vocational approach. From 1933:

The four year liberal arts college is facing a problem
which has a two-fold aspect, and which is becoming
more acute each year. The number of Junior Colleges
is increasing and there is a tendency for many students
to take their first two years of college work at a Junior
College. At the same time there is a growing tendency
for students who enter a four-year college to drop out
at the end of their Sophomore year and enter a
professional school where they try to carry their
college work and professional work at the same time.
So the regular four-year college is in danger of falling
between the upper and nether mill stones. It is well for
the Trustees to recognize that there is such a problem.

110

The only solution of it that I can see is for us to make and to keep Davidson so far superior to any Junior College that good students will recognize the difference, and at the same time to make it keep it better than the undergraduate work of the Universities. There will always be a large place for an institution like Davidson if we will keep our educational standards and our Christian ideals high. This we are trying to do. (14)

Davidson felt these pressures in its attempts to recruit students, efforts that were hampered by the more practical bent in high school education. From 1937:

The educational leaders in a number of states distinctly state that in formulating the curricula for high schools they are not thinking especially of preparing students for colleges and universities but for life. High school curricula are being more and more devoted to so-called practical and vocational subjects. As a result, high school graduates come to college with very little knowledge of the English language, or any other language, and very little knowledge of Algebra or Arithmetic. Back of all this lies the additional fact that the majority of our public school teachers are being trained in Teachers Colleges where more stress is laid upon methods and less upon content. (15)

The issue of pre-professional training was re-examined in 1938,
A re-study of the curriculum was the second step in the Movement. This was to see if Davidson's academic record has kept pace with the progress being made in the field of education, to scrutinize again the pre-professional training, and to see if Davidson is still turning out men adequately trained to assume positions of responsibility and constructive leadership in church, in society, and in the professional life of the community in which they are to live. (15)

111

But Davidson resisted the pressure and emerged from the depression with their identity as a college focused on the liberal arts intact and retains that focus today.

Citations

1. Lees-McRae College Catalog, 1931-32.
2. Lees-McRae College, *Pinnacles,* February 1932.
3. Lees-McRae College, *Pinnacles,* June/July 1932, *The Lees-McRae Game Farm.*
4. Lees-McRae College Catalog, 1938-39.
5. Louisburg College President's report to BOT, A.D. Wilcox, June 10, 1937.
6. *Louisburg College Bulletin,* Annual Report Number Vol. 1, Number 2, May 1940.
7. Campbell College President's report to BOT, L. Campbell, June, 1938.
8. *Wake Forest College Alumni News*, December, 1937, Vol. 7, No. 2, *New Physical Education Course Carrying Degree Credit to be Offered Prospective High School Coaches.*
9. Lees-McRae College – Faculty Minutes, January 5th, 1934.
10. Lees -McRae College Catalog, 1935-36.
11. *Wake Forest College Alumni News*, March, 1935, Vol. 4, No 3, *Degree Requirement changes Announced.*
12. Lees-McRae College, *Pinnacles,* January 1937, XXVI, *Education That Counts.*
13. Lees-McRae College, *Pinnacles,* May 1933, XXI, #5, *Can You Give a Job?*
14. Davidson College, President's Report to BOT, W. Lingle, 5th November.
15. Davidson College, President's Report to BOT, W. Lingle, 15th February, 1933.
16. Davidson College, Treasurer's Report, F.L. Jackson, 16 February 1938.

Chapter 10—Stiff Your Creditors

The colleges varied greatly in the impact debt had on their depression years. Debt was not an issue then for Lees-McRae College; the college had a long abhorrence of indebtedness, and refused to borrow money or mortgage any property. From 1932:

> Mr. Tufts further said that the Trustees would rather close than be harnessed by a debt, and that he would inform the Faculty each month as to financial conditions. (1)

Reaffirmed later in 1935:

> After the reading of the minutes, there arose a discussion of the wording of the charter, giving Trustees power of mortgaging, selling, etc. the physical property of the Institution. It was moved… seconded, and unanimously carried, that a resolution against mortgaging or going in debt in any way for the Association be incorporated by the Board in its by-laws. (2)

The annual audits of the four year colleges, Wake Forest (incomplete) and Davidson show no interest payment expenses, so these colleges likely had little concern about debt. Indeed, bonds and mortgages provided investment income in Davidson's endowment:

> Our real estate mortgage investments earn 6% and should produce an annual yield of approximately $47,000. During the last twelve months we have collected $43,250, leaving $3,500 more unpaid interest accounts than we had this time last year. The amount of uncollected interest on our books on November 1st this year is $29,870 as contrasted with $26,290 on the same date last year. During the past twelve months we have collected about 5 ½% on our mortgage loans. (3)

Campbell College, though the records are scarce, apparently had some struggles with debt, as evidenced by this 1931 letter to President Campbell from Jefferson Standard Life Insurance:

Dear Sir,

We regret that the extension which we are willing to grant on the $1000 curtailment due on this loan January 21st is unsatisfactory. Our Committee is unwilling to extend the note beyond April 1st. If payment cannot be made at that time, we will necessarily have to take legal action.

As to the interest note of $210, we shall expect payment in full on the due date. (4)

Campbell still had debt payments by the end of the depression – in 1939 their debt payments were $8,552 and payment of salaries owed to faculty of $907 out of total expenses of $108,000 (about 9% of the expense budget for that year).

The archives of Louisburg College amply record the struggle that institution had in dealing with debt through the depression years. Louisburg began building up a significant debt prior to the depression; $75,000 worth of bonds were issued in 1924 (maturing between 1929 and 1943) to pay for enlarging facilities and building an endowment (5). Apparently, during the 1920's it made financial sense to borrow money that would then be placed in the endowment.

The college borrowed even more money - $125,000 – in 1927 to pay off the old debt and finish paying for facilities improvement and a new heating plant. (6) At the time, college enrollment was growing, and the Board of Trustees apparently had little fear that the college would be unable to retire its debt.

When the new president of the college, C.C. Alexander took office in 1929 he faced a total indebtedness of $158,000, about four times the annual budget of the college. (7) The financial situation was dire; the Board authorized spending endowment funds to pay critical operating expenses:

In its November, 1929 meeting, the Board of Trustees authorized a committee to use money given to the college by Mr. B.N. Duke and deposited in various banks to apply to the payment of notes held by those banks against the college, and to apply the surplus to the payment of **most urgent bills** against the college… (7)

The situation with enrollment and debt worsened during the harsh environment of 1930, as detailed by Alexander in his report to the Board of Trustees:

Conditions as I Found Them

Within a short time after taking office I discovered two rather disturbing conditions in connection with the affairs of the College. First, I found that the indebtedness of the institution ran into the high figures of more than $160,000, which was approximately twice what it had been represented to me before I accepted office. Second, I found the enrollment, which had been reported through the press as a "record enrollment" to show a decrease of about one hundred from the year before. An estimate showed that if operations should continue throughout the year on the basis they had been started, the expenditures would exceed the revenue by more than $25,000.

Efforts to Improve Conditions

With this condition confronting us, we immediately instituted a program of strict economy, cutting expenses at every reasonable possible point. The result of precaution in finances we came through the year with a deficit in operations of only $15,642 instead of the $25,000, as is evidenced by the report of the audit which is before you…

With the heavy indebtedness resting upon the College and some of the creditors entering suit, the situation seemed impossible. I called a meeting of

115

the Executive Committee of the Board of Trustees and laid the situation before it. At this meeting… it was decided to appeal to the Board of Education of the North Carolina Conference to cooperate in the effort to find some relief.

As a result of this appeal the Board of Education… passed the following resolutions:

> 1. That… it is the opinion of the Board that under the existing circumstances the Trustees would be justified in using money given by the late Mr. B.N. Duke and belonging to the endowment, such money now being on deposit in banks, to pay the notes given to the banks and use whatever surplus may exist for the payment of any urgent bills of the institution…

Following up this action Mr. W.E. White and C.C. Alexander withdrew $40,000 with interest from the various banks and paid off notes of these banks to the aggregate amount of $32,000 with interest. The disposal of the remainder of this money and $10,000 in College bonds, which was included as part of the money given by Mr. Duke, is recorded in detail in the following report…. (*long list of creditors follows-all non-bank debts under $1,000*)

Another Crisis Arises

Matters ran along fairly smoothly through the winter until spring.

With the $5,000 in bonds maturing March 1, 1930 and the failure of the Farmers and Merchants Bank of Louisburg in early April, the College was confronted with another financial crisis and did not have funds available for operation…

…the Trustees of the College acting upon the approval of the Commission authorized the **execution of a loan** with Simmons and Harris, Inc., to the amount of $55,000, and that five hundred shares of the Tomlinson Chair Manufacturing Company, of High Point, NC, be pledged as security for the loan and that a deed of trust

116

be given on real estate owned by the College, located in Durham, NC, as additional security...

Prospects for the Future

Estimated Net Income from Students for 1930-31	$35,000
Estimated Income from Other Sources	$6,500
Total Estimate Income	$41,500

Estimated Operating Expenses	
Faculty Salaries including all employees	$31,000
Light, water and heat	$4,000
Food Supplies	$13,000
Interest on Bonds	$4,000
Maturing Bonds	$5,000
Interest on Toler Loan	$3,000
Insurance	$2,000
Office expenses	$5,000
Laundry, Students, Dining Hall and Infirmary	$1,500
Total	$68,800

It is evident from the above report that without financial assistance from some source, it will be impossible for the College to meet its operating expenses and carry its indebtedness. There seems to me to be two major causes for this crisis. **One is the load of the heavy indebtedness**. **The other is the financial condition prevailing in the territory from which the College draws its students**... I confess, however, that I do not see the solution to the present crisis unless there shall be forthcoming some financial aid. (8)

So, by the end of 1930, most of the endowment money had been spent and more money had been borrowed, using stocks held in the endowment as collateral. Total interest payments were $12,000 of an annual expense budget of $69,000 (over 17% of the annual budget).

The discouraged tone of his 1930 report foreshadows this development in the spring of 1931:

> To the Board of Trustees of Louisburg College:
> In view of and in consideration of the following facts, namely:
> First, that soon after my election to the presidency of Louisburg College on September 5, 1929, after the opening of the college year, and my assuming the duties of the office on September 10, 1929, I discovered and revealed to this Board the conditions pertaining to a heavy decrease in enrollment and the very large indebtedness of the College, amounting to more than $160,000.00; conditions which were so deplorable that it was realized that it would be virtually impossible to save the institution.
> Second, that we have labored together for nearly two years in an endeavor to overcome the insurmountable difficulties and solve the critical financial problems of Louisburg College without avail. During this period the aid of every agency, board, organization and individual known to offer any possibility of hope has been solicited without material results.
> Third, that your Board in-session at the College on January 13, 1931, elected a committee to investigate the possibility of continuing the operation of Louisburg College after this school year, which committee met and thoroughly canvassed the situation and found no hope for such continued operation...
> I hereby respectfully submit my resignation from the presidency of Louisburg College and kindly request that you accept the same to become effective June 1, 1931. (9)

After Alexander resigned, A. D. Wilcox took over as president of Louisburg College, presumably with a more accurate idea of the financial straits the institution faced, and projected a more positive tone, as evidenced by this 1931 report to the Board:

To take care of the matured bonds and interest on bonds and other forms of pressing indebtedness, I am putting on a quiet campaign of letters and interviews with selected prospects. This campaign will not attract much publicity and will occasion no pressure on preachers or churches of the Conference. I have had a few interviews already and feel very much encouraged concerning them… From the financial statement above it seems quite clear to me we will be able to operate the School upon the income from students this year. In addition to receipts from this source we are pressing the collection of bills receivable and notes receivable from former patrons of the School. We will secure a few thousand dollars from this source…

The owners of bonds and our other creditors are receiving our statements and letters and in almost every case we have encouraging responses indicating that we will have a very reasonable extension of time in taking care of old debts…

There are no major difficulties except those occasioned by the defaulted bonds and interest for the past year… Feeling seems to be widespread and deep seated that we are in the beginning of an era which may well be called the New Louisburg College. (10)

Louisburg College, as well as many other businesses and institutions, was successfully using another tactic for dealing with onerous debt - negotiating for extensions on debts, loan and bond payments. The new president spells out the college's financial situation to its creditors in a lengthy letter he mailed out shortly after assuming office. The original, unedited draft is reproduced below, with paragraphs that were later deleted in the final draft:

TO OUR CREDITORS:
Although this is a mimeographed letter it is highly personal and it deals with the financial situation in

Louisburg College and therefore has a direct bearing upon your business. It is put in this form for the sake of economy. After you have read it, I shall hope to receive an immediate answer on the points suggested below.

During the year I have written you stating it was my hope and expectation to pay within the year every bill originating since June 1, 1931. Our income from students as shown on our books seems to make this certain. From September 9, 1931 to the middle of March our collections were good. Our records show that out of $21,000 due during the period from September 9 to January $5,458.80 remained unpaid. The same people who made that record of payment are on our books charged with $19,000 for the second semester, January 20 to May 24. Of this amount $10,192.21 has been paid to date. This leaves a total of $13,457.32 now due from students on this year's business. Our obligations remaining due and unpaid for the current scholastic year, September 9, 1931 to May 24, 1932, are: salaries and wages, $8,353.85; merchandise and advertising, $6,691.33; total, $15,045.13. It will be seen that our bills receivable are only $1,587.86 less than our bills payable. In addition to money spent on current expenses we have paid $5,735.35 on debts incurred before my administration began, June 1, 1931. It is therefore clear that with full collections we would have closed the college year with $4147.99 as the net gain.

Our failure to collect at least 90%, of the accounts due us is not due to neglect, tack of industry, nor bad management, but to the **unprecedented scarcity of ready cash throughout the country and particularly is it noticeable in the eastern section of North Carolina**, the agricultural section. It is not due to the unwillingness to pay on the part of our patrons, nor of any desire to defraud the School. On the other hand, the money is owed to us by the highest type citizens in

120

this State. They tell us they will continue their payments in monthly installments until their accounts are fully settled. Many of them are giving short time notes due September 1, bearing interest payable in advance. Many of these notes will be paid in full. Others will be extended upon curtailment.   We will not lose a very large portion of the total amount now due us, but we will be delayed from- three to six months in collecting a large part of it. A small part will come in through the summer.

I am bringing this situation directly to the attention of about fifty of our friends who are able to help us in some measure by direct gifts.

This School has made such an advance in attendance and enrollment and has developed such an interest in this year of reorganization and revival that we are already assured of an enrollment next year at least 50% greater than this year. It may reach 100%. All indications point in that direction. With the income of such an enrollment added to the income from the collections named above, we shall be able to continue next year with a margin above the operating expenses sufficient to pay every dollar due on this year's business, plus 25% of the amounts still remaining due on old debts made prior to June 1, 1931. These facts recorded in our books and submitted to the annual meeting of the Board of Trustees on Tuesday, May 31, 1932, are herewith submitted to you in order that you may have sufficient information to guide you in determining what your policy will be concerning the account we owe you.

[The following was removed from final copy]
In my judgment there are only two courses possible. The first is for you to press your claims in the courts. This, of course, would precipitate bankruptcy procedure. This means the closing of the School and the loss of any further collections due us and the giving up of our chance to make this School a successful

financial as well as a successful educational Institution. With the closing of the School, the assets now standing at more than half a million will crumble to almost nothing because of the fact that the property cannot be used for any other purpose than as a School according to the reversion clause in the deed. By this method you could hope to collect only a very small percent of your account. I don't know how much. Hardly enough to pay legal costs. We will not close the School unless we're forced to because we believe we can win. We know we can.

The second course, and the one which I hope you will adopt, is to extend the time required for the payment of our account with you six months, allowing us to make monthly payments in the proportion in which we shall receive money due us. (end of deleted material)

I am sorry we are compelled to ask for this extension of time and I would not do it now unless I felt sure that with the conditions named above we would be able to pay every dollar we owe you and continue to do business with you on a larger scale and with better chance of paying more promptly another year. My information is that many business firms, factories, and even financial institutions, and many other Schools, are in the "red" as we are, but they are not closed. We have improved our condition during the most critical year in half a century. Let us alone for six months more and we will raise our credit with you. This doesn't mean that you will receive nothing for six months, but it does mean that we will have paid your entire bill by that time with installments.

Will you kindly give me an immediate answer stating what course you will pursue so that we may set our course accordingly. With very best wishes and the sincerest appreciation of your courtesies and consideration during the past year, I am

Very cordially yours,

Armour David Wilcox, President (11)

The deleted paragraphs contain another important tactic used in dealing with creditors – the threat of significant loses if the college declared bankruptcy. Loses might be avoided if more time were available to the college. Wilcox decided not to include that argument in the final letter, though the college did use it with other creditors later in the depression. The letter concludes with a more positive tactic – the prospect of continued business with helpful creditors when conditions improve.

Soliciting donors to increase charitable giving, mentioned by Wilcox in his report to the Board and his letter to creditors, met with little success. A copy of the president's letter of appeal to Mrs. Duke, wife of a pre-eminent philanthropist in North Carolina, was sent in 1932:

...When I took hold of the School in June, I found it was embarrassed by a multitude of notes and bills payable for merchandise. These debts had been accumulating for several years. In order to keep the confidence of our creditors and, in some cases, prevent legal action, I paid about twenty percent of this total miscellaneous indebtedness. This amount, of course, has to be taken from our operating income as we have no other source of revenue. Since the expenses of this year are almost exactly equal to the income from the students and patrons, this debt paying gives us an apparent deficit equal to the amount paid on old debts. The total debt is not increased. It is almost imperative, highly necessary to say the least, that this five thousand dollars should be secured in some way. This is in order to completely stop the demand that the School be closed. This literally means that five thousand dollars as a donation from the friends of the School will save Louisburg College now and, I think, forever. With the on-going of the School under the favorable circumstances now existing, the entire bonded debt and the merchandise debts may be refinanced without loss to a single creditor.

Now, Mrs. Duke, I appeal to you to aid us in this crisis. The sum of money asked for is very small in contrast to the scores of thousands of dollars contributed by Mr. Duke, but because of his great generosity in the past and the good built upon it, this five thousand dollars will make secure and permanent his benefactions. I have attempted to raise this money in a general solicitation of many people, but economic conditions are such that ordinary people have little or no means to give, although they wish to. It is our only hope that generous people of wealth will come to our rescue now.

Our Board of Trustees will meet on Monday, May 23. I am exceedingly anxious to present a report that will completely smother all remaining fears for the life of the School. This five thousand dollars will balance our budget, keep us on good terms with our creditors, and put a fire of enthusiasm in our crowd that will advance Louisburg College to the top as the greatest junior college in the Carolinas.

May I plead with you to think and pray your way through the situation disclosed in this letter? We need you.

With every good wish and high personal regards for you and your family, I am

Very sincerely yours,

Armour David Wilcox President (12)

Wilcox outlines another of the universal tactics debtors employ to keep functioning during hard times, namely pay a small portion of what is owed (in this case 20% of the debts owed to local merchants). Making some payments gave creditors hope that the college might still be able to eventually pay all its debts.

When appeals for donations failed, the college had little choice but to continue borrowing money by issuing more bonds. From a solicitation letter later the same year:

124

...Our collections which should have yielded at least ten thousand dollars in normal times and from which we expected at least seven thousand this year have amounted to about two thousand. This leaves us from five to ten thousand dollars short of what we actually need to pay out. I am sending you a copy of a letter which we are sending our patrons so you may see how we are attempting to collect the accounts. Now, Mr. Cooper, I have never directly asked you for assistance. We have $3,100 in Louisburg College bonds, paying six per cent interest – three one-thousand units and one one-hundred unit. These bonds are secured by first mortgage on the entire plant and of course, with the continued operation of the school, are worth par value. The interest is payable semi-annually, March 1 and September 1. If you would take over some are all of these bonds, it would do more than anything in sight to help us over this very critical period. As you know our prospects for next year are excellent. We can succeed, but I must find some way to handle our creditors who have supplied us with this year's merchandise. We need $10,000 awfully bad. If you can help us in any portion of this, I shall consider you a friend in deed because you will be a friend in need. Our people are so desperately hard up that even good payers in normal times cannot pay their own living expenses now.... (13)

The president's tone is much less optimistic in this stark appeal than his sanguine tone of the previous year.

The issue of debt and how to repay it continued to dominate the Board meetings for the next several years. The level of indebtedness continued to increase for the next year,

...The liabilities of the school are as follows, bonded indebtedness, $66,900; accrued past due interest on bonds, $16,847; merchandise indebtedness $33,477;

mortgage on Durham lot, $50,000; salaries to teachers, $13,557; totaling, $180,781. (14)

but it appears to have peaked around that time.

By 1935, Louisburg College had begun making efforts to address the debt problem. The college had preserved a lengthy correspondence with American National Insurance (ANI), who held bonds from the college worth $12,500, from 1935 to 1938. The correspondence is a largely complete record of how the college dealt with one of its largest creditors as Louisburg attempted to reduce the money it would have to repay them, and ANI's resistance to the college's efforts. (15)

August 31, 1935 From AD Wilcox to H. Beissner of
ANI
Dear Mr. Beissner,
The Board of Trustees of Louisburg College received a
very interesting report from a special committee which
had been appointed to make plans to pay the capital
debt on the College...
You will see that further action will be taken in
October and later in November at the session of the
NC Conference of the Methodist Church, South, which
is the owner of Louisburg College.
I feel quite sure that a definite plan will be formed and
that there will be action upon this matter at that time.
With thanks for the uniform courtesy that you have
shown the College in its years of distress, I am
Very Sincerely Yours,
A.D. Wilcox

February 8, 1936 From AD Wilcox to H. Beissner of
ANI
I am writing this letter to give you up to date
information concerning our movements looking toward
the payment of our bonded indebtedness.
A joint committee of six men chosen from the Board
of Christian Education of the NC Conference of the

ME Church, South, and the Board of Trustees of Louisburg College has been called to meet on two occasions. Each time the meeting was prevented on account of sickness or heavy winter storms. Up to date no meeting has been held. The most important member of the committee has gone to Florida for a month in order to recuperate. He will not return until about the first week in March...

The condition of the school is steadily improving. The prospects for the largest enrollment in the history of the school are excellent for the term 1936-37. Our new self-help plan has, I think, assured Louisburg College of a great future. The bonded indebtedness is the only real obstacle to success...

Believing that you will understand that the delay in this meeting is beyond our control and that you are willing to co-operate with us in the final settlement of this troublesome matter, I am...

The College seemed to be in no great hurry to formulate a concrete proposal. From August 1935 through April, 1936 nothing substantive was forthcoming.

April 9, 1936 From R. C. Weaver, Bond Department ANI to AD Wilcox.

Dear Sir:

In your favor of February 8th you advised that immediately upon the return of Dr. Flowers there would be a meeting called, at which meeting you would attempt to formulate a definite plan for the liquidation of the indebtedness of your college.

May we have your cooperation to the extent of a reply advising the results of the meeting as well as any other pertinent information with respect to this matter.

Yours very truly,

April 16, 1936 From A.D. Wilcox to R.C. Weaver

Gentlemen:

…Yesterday a strong committee representing the
North Carolina Conference and Louisburg College laid
plans for the liquidation of our bonded indebtedness.
Full information will be laid before you within a
month. It takes time for us to organize our campaign
and get down to business.
I am happy to say that the chances are very fine for the
payment of this debt.
I wish to thank you for the very considerate and
courteous treatment which you have given us.
With very best wishes, I am…

Still nothing through July, 1936.

July 20, 1936 From R.A. Patout, Bond Dept. ANI to
A.D. Wilcox
Dear Sir:
We expected some plan of refinancing for the
Louisburg College to have been presented about June.
Since we have had no word after your letter of April
16th, we are asking if you may not be able to supply
additional information at this time. We are indeed
interested in the financial progress of your institution
and hope that more permanent plans of settlement of
the bonded indebtedness may be forthcoming at this
time.

July 23, 1936 From A.D. Wilcox to R.A. Patout
Gentlemen:
…Since my letter of April 16 the Committee has begun
its work in contacting our creditors and in soliciting
funds with which to arrive at a settlement of our
obligations. The plan has already been formed. It is of
a dual nature. First, we are attempting to discover
upon what compromise basis settlement can be made;
second, we are attempting to raise a sufficient amount
of money which will finally be agreed upon.

It is considered impossible for us to pay our entire debt at 100% on the dollar. It will not be very long now, I think, until you will receive communication from the authorized committee of the Board of Trustees of Louisburg College concerning a proposition to take care of our matured bonds and interest.

It will interest you to learn that Louisburg College is making real progress in recovery. For instance, the enrollment for the year 1935-36 was 170% larger than the enrollment of 1930-31 – the year when the college was advertised to close its doors. Last year's enrollment was 67% larger than the enrollment of 1934-35. For two years the college has not sustained a deficit in its operating budget. Advance room reservation to date – July 23 – is 60% larger than on this date a year ago. This ratio of increase indicates that the College will be crowded to capacity and students will be turned away for lack of room to accommodate them.

The clear meaning of all this is that the remarkable success of the College operating under its new plan will make it easier to secure money with which to pay the old and destructive debt. It also means that those creditors who have given us the opportunity to work out this plan of recovery will fare much better than they could possibly have done if the College had been liquidated in 1931.

We are, therefore, very grateful to you and other creditors who have patiently waited until we could find a way to do what seemed at the time to be an impossible thing. Naturally the progress is slow as it involves a great many moves and the interviewing of a great many people.

Still believing that we are destined to win out in the project and that our creditors will be benefited by our efforts, I am...

July 27, 1936 From R.A. Patout, Bond Dept. ANI to
A.D. Wilcox
Dear Sir:
The mention in your letter of July 23rd of continued
progress of enrollment and advanced room
reservations was indeed grateful. We feel as you do
that the tide has turned and that your institution will be
in a position shortly to make a satisfactory proposition
for settlement of its indebtedness.
We extend to you our best wishes for continued
improvements and request that you keep us posted as
to any late developments.

Unfortunately, the archives contains no copies of the
actual plan submitted to ANI, however, the remaining
correspondence gives a fairly clear picture of the proposal. The
college proposed to repay 75% of the principal owed, with no
payment of interest on the bonds.

October 28, 1936 From R.A. Patout, Bond Dept. ANI
to A.D. Wilcox
Dear Sir:
We are in receipt of your letter and plan dated October
20th and wish to assure you that this Company is
desirous of cooperating in every manner possible.
However, we feel that acceptance of the Plan could be
more easily secured when presented to our Finance
Committee if we knew that this had already been given
approval by other bondholders.
Accordingly, we would appreciate your furnishing us
with names of certain other institutional bondholders
with whom we might correspond in reference to the
proposed Plan of Debt Readjustment. Also, we would
appreciate your sending us a summary statement of
late operating figures of the College, as well as a
statement of assets and liabilities…

In other words, ANI wanted to be certain that they were being treated equitably relative to other creditors of Louisburg College. Equitable treatment would appear to be a critical tactic in dealing with creditors.

November 2, 1936 From R.A. Patout, Bond Dept. ANI to A.D. Wilcox
Dear Sir:
Even though we have just written you on October 28th in reference to the proposed plan of Refinancing, we find one additional question we would appreciate your answering at this time.
According to the wording of the proposal – "and in consideration of the acceptance of the proposition embodied in said letter by other creditors we agree to accept 75%, etc." – **we infer that 100% acceptance of the proposal by bondholders and creditors would be necessary to declare the plan operative.**
If this is not the case, kindly inform us what percent is considered sufficient and what treatment might be given those who do not accept the proposal.

November 9, 1936 From A.D. Wilcox to R.A. Patout
Gentlemen:
In further reply to your letter we are submitting a list of the bond holders who have already accepted our proposition.
In answer to the question raised in your letter of November 2 as to the number of bond holders and creditors which would be necessary to declare the plan operative, we beg to advise that our Committee has not passed definitely upon this proposition. I think, however, that it is the sense of this Committee to submit the matter to the Conference upon the acceptance of our proposition in the amount of 75%. This would make it possible to put on our campaign without further delay, and in the hope that all will accept within due time. We are confident that our

131

proposition offers more to all the creditors than could possibly be obtained by court action or any other action or form of settlement, hence we are hoping to avoid this alternative.

We, therefore, hope that with the facts here presented before your committee its **unconditional acceptance of our proposition may be received prior to the convening of Conference on November 19**...

Information asked for in your letter of October 28, 1936

1. Auditor's Report as of June 30, 1936 mailed under separate cover... In this connections, allow me to state that the auditor's estimate of values is, in our opinion, accurate so long as the property is used for educational purposes but it should be taken into consideration that **should Louisburg College cease to exist a very different picture would be presented. The buildings would be practically a total loss. The Duke Endowment Fund, being conditional upon the continuation of the College would revert to the Duke Foundation and the Library and equipment would hardly be worth more than 25% of its value as estimated above. The sale value of the property at Louisburg, for other than educational purposes, would in the opinion of our Committee, be worth scarcely more than $35,000 or $40,000.**

3. Of 27 bond holders 14 have accepted our proposition in Full. 3 have expressed a desire for the par value of bonds but are willing to cancel all interest. 9 have not been heard from. Most of these are individual holders of small amounts.

An interesting change in the tempo of negotiations emerges here. The college took considerable time to come up with a concrete proposal, submitted the proposal in late October, and requested "unconditional" acceptance of the proposal within a month. The College appears to be attempting to control the pace of the negotiations, but ANI refused to follow the college's timetable.

November 13, 1936 From R.A. Patout to A.D. Wilcox
...We realize that you are making every possible effort to complete your arrangements before the Conference Meeting on November 19th, and hope that we may be in a position to cooperate with you. However, before we are able to give you a definite answer regarding our bonds, we must present the whole situation to our Finance Committee and await their action.

November 24, 1936 From R.A. Patout to A.D. Wilcox
As yet we have been unable to present your proposed plan of refinancing to our Finance Committee...
...we hope you may be able to supply us with certain additional information which we feel will materially assist our Committee in coming to a satisfactory conclusion as to what action to take with reference to our bonds. We are particularly anxious to know the number of bonds that have been placed under assent to your proposal and would also like to know the results of your meeting with the Church Conference on November 19th.

December 1, 1936 From A.D. Wilcox to R.A. Patout
Dear Mr. Patout,
...On Saturday, November 22 the North Carolina Annual Conference of the M.E. Church, South, in session at New Bern, N.C. adopted a resolution authorizing Louisburg College to make a campaign within the Church and among friends of the College to raise $65,000 for the purpose of liquidating the bonded and unsecured indebtedness...
Of the twenty-nine owners of bonds whose names we have secured seventeen have accepted the terms as stated in our circular letter of October 20. The total amount held by these seventeen owners is $21,000... I

133

believe that your Company holds $12,500 worth of bonds... It would appear that aside from the bonds held by your Company approximately fifty percent of the outstanding bonds are subject to the acceptance already received in our office...

Our campaign will get under way in the early part of January and we shall be glad indeed to have your reply as early as possible...

December 30, 1936 From H. Beissner (manager Bond Department) to A.D. Wilcox

Dear Sir:

We are preparing to approach our Finance Committee relative to your school's debt settlement proposal, but before doing so, we prefer securing the latest information available regarding the position other creditors have taken. According to your letter of December 1st, we note holders of $12,000 had refused the terms and other bondholders controlling approximately $22,000 had not yet been heard from. **Specifically, only holders of $21,000, or 32% of the outstanding issue, had accepted the Plan at that time and you can readily appreciate that this is a comparatively small figure when one attempts to convince a finance committee that the proposal is believed to be fair and equitable and has received favorable response from the interested bondholders.**

We shall appreciate hearing further from you, and if the information furnished us is sufficiently favorable, we shall approach our Committee immediately. Since we hold $12,500, or more than 18% of the total issue, we feel that our position in this matter is sufficiently important to insist upon the information requested.

January 9, 1937 – From A.D. Wilcox to H. Beissner
The requests in your letter are very fair and I am,
herewith, submitting all the information that we have
secured up to date.

1. The total amount of bonds accepted to date is
   $40,000
2. This is 60% of the total issue of
   $66,547
3. The total amount of tentative acceptances is
   $11,500
4. The total acceptances including the latter figure is
   $51,562
5. This is approximately 77% of the total bond issue.

….If your company accepts our proposition more than
96% of the total issue will be accounted for…

I have given these additional figures in order that you
may see that the creditors who are best informed
concerning our situation have considered our offer the
best that could be hoped for. The people who have not
accepted in some cases are expecting to do so; in other
cases, we believe, they have not received our letter or
have charged the amount off which was on their books
and hold nothing against us.

**It is only fair to say to you that we have brought
into consultation with many of the most eminent
and fair-minded men in North Carolina including
college executives, bankers, business men and the
presiding Bishop… These men without a single
exception have repeatedly stated that the terms we
offer are the best that the College could possibly
make** and that the amount we are undertaking to raise
is undoubtedly the maximum amount which could be
raised in this Conference for this purpose.

**It is also worthy of note that a sister college in this
neighborhood, which is about twice as large as
Louisburg College and a four year standard college,
has liquidated its bonded indebtedness at twenty-
five cents on the dollar and its unsecured debt at**

three cents on the dollar. It is also a fact that Lake Junaluska, a half million dollar concern owned by the Southern Methodist Episcopal Church, has liquidated its debt of $350,000 for $100,000 which is less than 33%. Many other institutions in this section have liquidated at various figures, and so far as I know Louisburg College is making the best offer that has been made by any other institution. I trust that the facts related in this letter will be sufficient to lead your committee into an acceptance of our offer.

From this letter, we get a clear picture that debt default was relatively widespread during these years.

February 6, 1937 – From A.D. Wilcox to H. Beissner
…The North Carolina Conference of the Methodist Episcopal Church, South, has authorized this campaign conditioned upon the acceptance of all of our creditors. **They decline to attempt to raise any money at all unless they are assured that the money which is raised will liquidate the debt entirely.** It is, therefore, absolutely necessary to know your will upon this matter before the meeting of our general committee which will take place on or about February 19 or 20th. Your acceptance, therefore, of our proposition will guarantee starting the campaign. **On the other hand your rejection of our proposition would prevent even the starting of this campaign**. This is in accordance with the conditions stated in writing that were agreed upon by the College and the proper officials of the North Carolina Conference.
…Again stating our appreciation of the fine courtesy which your Company has shown to us and expressing the hope that we may have an early answer from you…

Again, the college applies pressure to ANI – they threaten that the college will not try to raise the money unless it will pay off the debt in full. ANI responded rather sharply to this tactic.

February 8, 1937 – From K.I. Fosdick Treasurer, ANI to A.D. Wilcox

We have patiently watched the correspondence that has passed between this office and your College and have been extremely hopeful that when times became more favorable your institution would be in a position and also willing to carry out its bonded indebtedness. Of course, we realize that all over the Country obligations have been reduced, but in your particular case, owing to the size of your debt, it is our feeling that if your College should continue to exist, then the money that you owe the first mortgage bondholders should ultimately be paid in full.

We do not want to be arbitrary in this matter and fully appreciate all the difficulties you have encountered and your desire to get rid of as many obligations as possible, but in reviewing many cases of a somewhat similar nature, it has been our opinion that where the debt is not too large and the future is not too black, the creditors should feel justified in asking for an extension program which will permit full payment over a period of years.

As I stated before, we want to give you every consideration in this matter and have this letter back in your hands before you start your campaign.

Therefore, this is the Company's position - **we do not favor ideas of reduction of principal. As stated above, we believe that where an institution has to continue, the secured indebtedness against it must be cared for to the satisfaction of the cooperating creditors.**

I need not comment upon the extremely generous attitude that the bondholders have taken for the past five years or more, during which your College has

been given an opportunity to work out your financial problem.
Very truly yours…

Shortly after this, A.D. Wilcox traveled to Galveston, TX, home of ANI, to negotiate a settlement in person. He sickened and died shortly after returning from the trip.

March 11, 1937 – From E.H. Malone Sec. Board of Trustees to K.I. Fosdick, ANI

It is with deep regret that we have to advise you that Mr. A.D. Wilcox, President of Louisburg College, died after an illness of a few days on March 9. Mr. Wilcox was taken sick upon the trip back from Galveston where he had conferred with you in regard to liquidation of the Louisburg College bonds held by your Company, and his condition was such upon his return here that it was impossible for any of the College officials to discuss the result of this conference.

Figure 24: A.D. Wilcox, President of Louisburg College, 1933.

…we would appreciate very much your advising us of the result of the conference between Mr. Wilcox and your officials at the time of his late visit…

March 15, 1937 – From K.I. Fosdick Treasurer, ANI to E.H. Malone

We were indeed regretful to learn of Mr. A. D. Wilcox's passing and hasten to extend our sympathies. Relative to the debt adjustment proposal under consideration, this matter was submitted to our Finance Committee immediately following Mr. Wilcox's visit and our Finance Committee took the position that we stand ready to waive all past due and accumulated interest provided we are paid 100 cents on the dollar of the principal amount. This information is being handed to you promptly so that due consideration may be given our position at your Board Meeting to be held March 18th.

We shall appreciate hearing from you following the meeting in question.

July 1, 1937 From W.O. Watson, Asst. Treas. ANI to E.H. Malone, Louisburg College.

The file concerning the above bonds has been handed me for attention, in view of the fact that letters addressed to you under date of March 15th, May 10th and June 17th, have not received the courtesy of a reply.

This Company is the owner of $12,500 in the bonds issued against the College, this being some 18% of the total issue, and therefore we feel that we should be advised of any action taken relative to the refunding of the debt of payment in full. I realize that we have rejected the proposition which was formerly submitted to us by the late Mr. Wilcox, but certainly subsequent to the rejection of that proposition your board has taken some action regarding the debt.

This Company felt that the proposition made by us to Mr. Wilcox and as set forth to you in our letter of March 15th, was not unfair to the College. It is not our desire to create a nuisance value on our bonds, as is evidenced by our heretofore co-operative attitude regarding the debt and we are at this time asking that we be definitely advised as to what progress is being made by you in making arrangements for payment of bonds and interest due thereon, or in attempting to work out some proposition for re-writing the loan in its entirety.

I am going to request that you give us some immediate information, and if same is not forth-coming, other steps will have to be taken to secure advice on the

139

bonds, and the matter then referred to our Finance
Committee for proper action to protect our interests.

August 3, 1937 From D.E. Earnhardt, Pres. Louisburg
College to W.O. Watson, ANI
...I have been out of the office the greater part of the
time recently engaged in work on the campaign to raise
money for the College, hence your failure to hear from
us.
...It is my understanding that all of our bond owners,
except your Company, have agreed to accept the
settlement offered by the Trustees...
One of the conditions of acceptance incurred by the
creditors was that all of the creditors of a class would
be paid the same percentage of their claims settlement
thereof and that a settlement would be tendered by
December 31st, 1937. In our preliminary canvass of
the field we have found that many of the prospective
donors express a reluctance to cooperate at all until it
is definitely understood that the indebtedness of the
College will be fully retired. You can see the position
in which the Trustees are placed. Hence, it was the
sense of the Board and so resolved that all creditors of
a class would be treated alike and that unless there was
a sufficient amount raised to retire the entire
indebtedness on the plant proper all contributions
would be refunded....
Your Company – as well as the vast majority of other
creditors of Louisburg College – has been very lenient
and generous and there has been no disposition on the
part of the Trustees to dictate terms nor to drive a hard
bargain. As a matter of fact, these Trustees, who have
labored for years in trying to save this Institution are
fully sensible to the moral obligation and after careful
appraisal of all the assets of the Institution and the
possibility of raising money, went the limit according
to what they thought was possible in making this a
compromise offer. If this plan does not work out as

anticipated it is my opinion that the sense of the Board
of Trustees will be to ask the Court, under Section 77B
of the Unites States Bankruptcy Act, to pass upon
some plan of reorganization or to dispose of the assets
under the College and distribute same among its
creditors.

**On account of a stipulation in the original grant of
the land upon which the College plant is situated
and by reason of legislative enactment, this
property can only be used for the purpose of
educating people of the white race. This
stipulation, while not effecting the potential value of
the College for such educational purposes, will of
course be a serious handicap in disposing of same
and I myself, as well as those in a better position to
know, am confident that the proposition offered by
the Trustees will net much more than could
possibly be hoped for through either voluntary of
involuntary liquidation in the courts.** In making
these statements I assure you that there is no implied
threat or disposition on my part to endeavor to force
upon you an acceptance of the proposition made by the
Trustees. I am simply stating frankly what I am
advised, and find, to be the facts.

Some of our creditors in agreeing to accept the offer of
the Trustees have indicated that they consider the
difference between the full value of their claims and
the amount received as gift and will ask for a reduction
in settlement of their income taxes accordingly. As
Louisburg College is a religious educational Institution
I know of no reason why such a reduction will not be
perfectly proper and legal. You will probably know
better than the writer as to this and I merely suggest
same for your consideration.

We realize very fully that however benevolent your
disposition may be in this matter you cannot feel the
interest in Louisburg College that the Trustees do; and
in considering this matter you may feel that our

statement of facts and opinion as to condition may be biased by our interest. If you have a representative in North Carolina we would be only too glad to have him make a thorough investigation of the situation, giving him access to all of our records to the end that you may have the benefit of his opinion... The Board of Trustees is hoping, and I think I may say without any desire to appear dramatic, earnestly praying that all the creditors of Louisburg College will agree to the acceptance of the proposed offer before the campaign is completed; and that as a result of the campaign that they may be able to carry out the plan of debt liquidation initiated by our beloved, deceased president, Mr. Wilcox....

October 12, 1937 From R.A. Patout to D.E. Earnhardt
Inasmuch as we have had no word from you for some time regarding recent developments in your College's activities, we would appreciate your communicating with us at your convenience regarding this, as well as any steps you may have considered toward readjusting the outstanding debt.

October 15, 1937 From D.E. Earnhardt to R.A. Patout
We are pushing forward with our campaign to liquidate our bonded indebtedness on Louisburg College. We are carrying this movement on through December of this year and will not be able to make final report until the last of that month.
We are still hopeful of success though the going at the present time is rather slow.

January 25, 1938 From D.E. Earnhardt to R.A. Patout
When you wrote to me a month ago I overlooked the fact that you requested a statement concerning recent developments at Louisburg College. Please pardon the delay...

During December we saw clearly that we were not going to succeed in raising the whole of the indebtedness. We wrote to the creditors asking them to give us an extension of ninety days on the agreement which they had signed. Practically all who signed that agreement consented to the extension. This extension terminates on March 31st of this year. It remains to be seen as to what will be our status on that date.

Counting cash and pledges we have secured enough to pay one-third of the very liberal discount agreed to by our creditors. We are not privileged to use this money until we have secured enough to wholly liquidate the debt. We are getting out a letter now, however, to donors asking their

Figure 25: D.E. Earnhardt, President of Louisburg College, 1938.

advice concerning the use of the money which they have given.

We are doing our best to raise money enough to pay all that we owe. It looks like a hopeless task. **Two former presidents of Louisburg College literally gave their lives in their efforts to free this Institution of the incubus of debt. Since coming here I have been able to see how it was that they could not stand the strain. The full realization is upon us that we are honor bound to pay what we owe, and yet we realize at the same time that we are not able to pay it. Those of us who are working at the debt had no hand in making it. In fact, we abhor the debt. That is the reason that we are so determined to do something about this one.**

In working and suffering over this thing, we are
working not simply for Louisburg College and the
North Carolina Conference but for our creditors as
well. Our creditors have helped us with their patience
and leniency and their generous offer to accept less
than we owe for the accounts. We have no right to
insist on it but we would be greatly assisted in this
monumental task if your Company could see fit to
come into the agreement which practically all of our
creditors have signed. The fact that you are not with us
in this hampers and embarrasses us in our efforts to
secure contributions. We acknowledge that we owe
every cent of these claims but we know that concession
on the part of the creditors is a great incentive to the
donors.
With appreciation for your past favors and thanking
you in advance for anything else which you may do to
help out In this case, I am...

January 26, 1938 From Walter Patten, NC Meth. Conf.
to ANI
The endeavor of the trustees of Louisburg College to
raise funds last summer to pay its bonded indebtedness
of $65,000 resulted in raising $10,500 in cash and
about as much more in pledges. This is rather
discouraging, but the task will be continued...
As you have indicated an unwillingness to accept the
75% plan for all of the bonds may we suggest a
substitute, namely, that we pay you 75% for the
matured bonds, and pay par for the unmatured bonds
as they become due March 1st but without interest.
This can be worked out on a five year plan. We hope
to receive your approval...

This compromise appears to have broken the logjam.
Acceptance quickly followed.

February 11, 1938 from K.I. Fosdick ANI to Walter Patten

This will confirm our telegram of today as follows:

YOUR PROPOSAL TO PAY 7,000 PAST DUE BONDS AT SEVENTY-FIVE PER CENT WITHOUT INTEREST AND REMAINING 5,500 AT MATURITY AT PAR WITHOUT INTEREST AGREEABLE WITH US."

It is our understanding that the cash now available is to be applied as payment on past due bonds at 75% of par value, without interest, and that this Company is to receive its proportionate share of such payments on our $7,000 bonds maturing through 3-1-38.

For our $5,500 bonds, not yet due, we are to be paid par, without interest, on the present maturities as follows;

$ 1,500 - 3/1/40
2,000 - 3/1/41
500 - 3/1/42
1,500 - 3/1/43

We sincerely trust that this action will enable your organization to go forward with the refinancing program...

February 14, 1938 From Walter Patten to K.I. Fosdick

Thanks for your acceptance of our proposal...

One final exchange of Louisburg College correspondence from the depression era that shows the human dimension of indebtedness:

Pres. D.E. Earnhardt
Louisburg College
Louisburg NC   Ahoskie, N.C.
                                April 16, 1938

Dear Sir:

I received your letter relative to seeing me about my daughter's education at Louisburg College. As yet, you have not paid me a visit.

As you already know, I invested $7,000 in Louisburg College Bonds and now the interest on that amount has not been paid since 1932. Now, that my girls are ready to enter College this fall, I need my money.

I am putting this proposition up to you. If you will educate my two daughters on the interest, which has accrued on the $7,000 since 1932 and then pay me the full $7,000, I will consider sending them to your college. If you will not do this, I will commence legal proceedings at once, as an attorney has already told me that I could collect the full amount with interest. This is a fair proposition, as I have received no income since 1932 and I know, you as a minister want to do the right thing by me, a widow with four dependent children.

As my money is invested in Louisburg College bonds and I am getting no income from them, I have to work on the W.P.A. and barely receive enough to feed and clothe my children. If I cannot educate them, they will not be able to take care of themselves.

Please let me hear from you at once.

Sincerely, Mrs. Hilda J Corwin

The total cost of sending a daughter to Louisburg College in 1938 was $227 per year. The $7,000 represented by the Louisburg bond represented about six years of a faculty salary at that time.

April 22, 1938

Mrs. Hilda J. Corwin, Ahoskie, North Carolina

My dear Mrs. Corwin:

I have been hoping that I might have an opportunity to be in your part of the state, either in the spring or summer, and talk with you concerning the plans for your daughters' education. I can tell you now that we will be very glad to have your daughters come here, and pay their entire expenses out of the bond money which we owe you. We are very anxious, in fact, to do that. As to whether they could get their expenses from the interest on those bonds, as you suggested, would have to depend upon the agreement made between you and Dr. Patten. Dr. Patten is in full charge of our bonded indebtedness, and he is the only one who can speak with authority on that phase of it.

You speak of an attorney who informed you that you could collect not only the $7000.00 principal, but accrued interest as well. We realize that we owe both the principal and the interest; but the thing that pains us immeasurably is our inability to pay what we owe. From what you said in reference to this, l judge that your attorney is not fully informed as to the principles involved in this bond settlement. The bonds are not worth any more than our ability to pay. The good will of the Methodist Church of North Carolina Is their only security, since the property on which they are based has a reversionary clause. We would not use this fact as a means to escape payment. **I am simply saying this to show that we do not have to pay anything on the bonds. Whatever we pay on them will just be because we feel our moral obligation, and our willingness to do our level best for our creditors**.

Dr. Patten and I both feel that we certainly ought to pay you a hundred cents on the dollar for your bonds. We wish to do that and we would like for you to help us do that by sending your children here, and letting

the cost of their education come out of this
indebtedness. I sincerely hope that you can do this
because it will enable us to pay you what we owe. I am
not sure that we can do it in any other way.
Assuring you of our warm personal regards and our
sincere desire to do the best possible for you and your
children, I am,
Yours sincerely,
D. E. Earnhardt
President (16)

There is no record of the final settlement with Mrs.
Corwin.

Citations

1. Lees-McRae College Faculty Minutes, 2nd February, 1932.
2. Lees-McRae College, Edgar Tufts Memorial Association Board of Trustees minutes, October 22nd, 1935.
3. Davidson College Treasurer's Report, F.L. Jackson, 8th November 1935.
4. Campbell College, letter from Jefferson Standard Life Insurance to J.A. Campbell, January 19, 1931.
5. *A History of Louisburg College – 1787-1958*, Miriam Russell, 1959 Thesis # 58028 Appalachian State University. p. 87.
6. *A History of Louisburg College – 1787-1958*, Miriam Russell, 1959 Thesis # 58028 Appalachian State University. p. 93.
7. *A History of Louisburg College – 1787-1958*, Miriam Russell, 1959 Thesis # 58028 Appalachian State University. p. 102.
8. Louisburg College, President's report to BOT, C.C. Alexander, September, 1930.
9. Louisburg College, letter to BOT, C.C. Alexander, 1931.

10. Louisburg College, President's report to Board of Trustees, A. D. Wilcox, November, 1931.
11. Louisburg College, Draft Letter to Creditors, A.D. Wilcox, May 31, 1932.
12. Louisburg College, Letter to Mrs. B.N. Duke, A. D. Wilcox, April 19, 1932.
13. Louisburg College, Letter to Colonel Wade H. Cooper, A. D. Wilcox, May 22, 1932.
14. Louisburg College, *A Brief for the Maintenance of Louisburg College*, 1933.
15. Louisburg College, American National Insurance sequence, 1935-38.
16. Louisburg College, Correspondence with Hilda J. Corwin, April 16, 1938.

Chapter 11—Conclusions

The five colleges experienced the depression differently. Davidson stayed its course – reaffirmed its mission as a liberal arts college and made no attempt to grow enrollment to meet the financial challenges they faced. Except for instituting a merit pay system and eliminating automatic pay raises, their faculty and administration weathered the times with little evidence of suffering. At the other extreme is Louisburg College. Faculty and administrative turnover was an on-going churn; debt was a consuming issue throughout the depression years, and remained a problem as the country emerged from the depression; student enrollment fell to the point where the institution's future was in serious doubt, but rebounded when the college dramatically reduced its fees. Lees-McRae, Campbell, Wake Forest and Louisburg generated new programs and ideas, many of them destined to be short-lived, but some succeeding and persisting. Wake Forest put its large population of alumni to work as recruiters to begin a sustained program of student growth that saw them through the depression. Campbell and Lees-McRae allowed students to pay with commodities.

What then can we learn from the struggles of these five North Carolina colleges through the Great Depression? Could the strategies and tactics that they employed be used in today's climate of economic turmoil?

All the colleges delayed construction and capital spending during the depression. This may not be so much a strategy as a reflection of the economic realities of the time, but there is no evidence that any of the colleges borrowed money to expand once the depression began. Several colleges suffered from their lack of capital spending – student housing space was an on-going problem for Davidson and Lees-McRae, but their students made do with what facilities were available. The lesson that their experience teaches us is that much of the capital spending is discretionary. Newer, more attractive and efficient facilities are assets, but an institution can survive and even flourish, for a time at least, without them,. By the late 1930's, as donors began to loosen their purse strings and charitable giving to the colleges improved, several colleges began addressing the issue of deferred construction and a building boom ensued on some campuses.

All the colleges except Davidson dramatically increased their enrollment through the depression. At the most economic level, this allowed them to "make up in volume" what they lost in individual profit, as they reduced the cost of attending college. If you do not incur higher costs associated with a larger student body, if, as Wake Forest phrased it, *"The College has practically all the physical equipment necessary to accommodate adequately this number, and it is of vital importance that she be successful in increasing the student body to this number,"* (1) then your bottom line will improve.

At a deeper level, the increase in the student body reaffirmed the purpose and higher mission of the college. As Lees-McRae and Wake Forest articulated in their external publications on numerous occasions, the institutions were growing, despite the hard economic times. The underlying message was that the colleges were relevant, that they provided a valuable service to their communities and to higher education in the state. This message probably strengthened external support of the institutions and fortified the faculty and staff as they labored there under heavy workloads often with poor pay.

All the colleges were conscious of the cost of an education during the depression. Even Davidson spent considerable time studying the issue in administrative and board meetings. After years of appreciable tuition and fee inflation, costs froze or dropped significantly during the depression. Both Lees-McRae and Louisburg tried to raise fees during the depression, but quickly abandoned their attempts, and in Louisburg's case, slashed costs dramatically. Where external publications survive in the archives, there is good evidence that the low cost of attending an institution was considered to be a major selling point (Wake Forest, Lees-McRae and Louisburg). Today, we seem to be seeing a similar shift in psychology as the economy contracts and attitudes towards debt begin to shift.

Less than two percent of the United States population work as full-time farmers today, so the practicality of trading a college education for produce or livestock is limited. In a service economy, most of the bartering opportunities are bartering for services. Trading labor for an education is alive and well; college work-study programs became wide-spread during the 1930's and are now an integral part of college planning for many families. Other bartering opportunities exist. Colleges have a variety of information technology needs – web page design and maintenance, network development and maintenance, software to run administrative databases, instructional software – and many of the basic needs remain – providing energy and light, maintaining grounds and buildings, printing and designing mailings and publications, providing a variety of student services – all of which are opportunities for enterprising families with little cash and/or access to credit.

Bartering was so widespread during the Great Depression because money was hard to come by. The dollar was backed by precious metal reserves, and the number of dollars in circulation was limited by these reserves. Today, the dollar is a fiat currency, with potentially no limit to the number in circulation. Many have argued convincingly (ex: Eric Janszen, http://www.itulip.com/) that a deflationary depression is impossible today. It does not necessarily follow though that those fiat dollars will be in the hands of every family who wants to send their children to college, especially if unemployment continues to rise. Bartering a college education for services may become more popular if family incomes continue to fall.

Salary cuts and pay freezes are cropping up more frequently in news stories today, and were a common feature in these colleges during the Great Depression. Faculty saw a good deal of salary compression at some schools, and pay was reduced to what was essentially a living wage at Lees-McRae and Louisburg. How the administration handled salary issues was probably more important than the actual amount cut. President Wilcox at Louisburg College told his employees, *"I am therefore not asking anyone to remain and have advised all of them to secure work elsewhere if they can possibly do it,"* (2) and the result was an almost complete turn-over of teaching faculty, and the loss of an immense amount of institutional memory and identity. From Lees-McRae College, in contrast, there is more of sense of shared hardship that helped retain an important core of long-term faculty and staff, *"When it seemed that this total reduction of twenty percent would not be sufficient to enable the college to meet its operating expenses, all of the employees, including faculty and teachers, voluntarily agreed to accept such remuneration as the income of the college might justify and that in the event the minimum salaries agreed upon should not be paid through this method the college should be relieved from all further obligations and that the debt would stand discharged."* (3) Management's handling of salary issues is critical to maintaining employee morale and loyalty.

The smaller colleges were also more paternalistic in those days – faculty were often provided housing at little or no cost (faculty were required to live on campus at Lees-McRae) and they dined at the college cafeteria – so the non-salary benefits made up for salary cuts to a certain extent. This is an avenue any organization could explore if salary cuts are unavoidable – can the organization provide other support to its employees at little cost to itself?

The disparity between faculty and administrative salaries and work-loads shrunk during the Great Depression. Administration took significant pay cuts and assumed more duties, often including teaching duties. This almost certainly strengthened the bonds of shared hardship, and strengthened the colleges.

Some colleges achieved a remarkable degree of self-sufficiency during the depression, largely feeding themselves with their farms, building and maintaining their own water systems and, in the case of Lees-McRae, maintaining their own hydroelectric plant for power. Recently, there seems to be an opposite trend in colleges, to outsource anything that is not directly related to instruction. Some colleges have sold their residence halls to companies that manage them, and that potential source of revenue has disappeared. Most colleges have contracts with large companies that run concessions, provide food services, provide maintenance and housekeeping and provide security for an annual fee. There are companies that develop and lease databases to colleges to advise them as to the best way to structure their financial aid packages for each of their students. Some colleges feel the necessity to pay outside consultants to help them screen and hire college presidents or other administrators. The inability (or unwillingness) of even small colleges today to conduct their own affairs would probably appall the college presidents and administrators who survived the depression years. If economic conditions continue to worsen, I predict that self-sufficiency will once again be seen as a virtue and "insourcing" will be a hot topic at administrative retreats.

The colleges that felt economic distress most strongly were the ones that showed the most willingness to innovate and diversity their program offerings. A case could be made that the financial pressures of the Great Depression spurred experimentation in curriculum and programs. Innovation was directional – the colleges responded to societal needs for practical, vocational training. *"No longer is a diploma a passport into success. To be of any value it must represent definite preparation for living. Today the world is demanding more of its young people than ever before. "We must drive home, once and for all, that it is the trained person in any field, the person who can use tools in the vocations or in handicraft who is the best asset of the country..."* (4)

Whether the topic was game bird management, scriptwriting or physical education, the movement was away from the generic liberal arts program toward applied degrees, though the colleges who adopted the vocational approach continued to stress the value of a liberal arts education, *"Vocations must be joined with a liberal education sufficient to give the student an understanding of his place in the world and the fullest opportunities of every single craft and occupation. The humanities, the social sciences, the physical sciences and the arts are as important for his development as any trade."* (5)

Colleges today are already innovating with on-line, distance programs and evening classes that allow students to work and continue their education. I would expect the pace of these changes in college programs to accelerate, and the pressure to accept non-traditional programs and degrees will continue to be felt by accrediting agencies.

Finally, we see how debt can affect the operation of colleges during times of economic strife. Indebtedness weighed heavily on Louisburg College throughout the depression decade and even beyond. The college owed money to local businesses, to distant bondholders and to its own employees. Debt ate up the college's endowment, some of which had ironically been built on borrowed money.

When dealing with creditors, Louisburg College adopted tactics that seem to be timeless and universal – pay the most critical bills first; pay small amounts to creditors if at all possible; encourage creditors to extend payments with the hope of future business when times improve; point out the loss that would follow bankruptcy, if deadlines are not extended; try to control the pace of negotiations about debt repayments (colleges have a distinct advantage here, since the tradition of shared governance ensures lots of slow, deliberate committee work); be scrupulously fair in your dealings with creditors, as no creditor wants to believe that their good will is being abused.

As in the Great Depression, our current economic ills result from an extended period of growing consumption and indebtedness for families and institutions. At the turn of the century, I attended a faculty meeting when a college president informed faculty and staff that we needed to change our thinking about debt, that debt was a "good thing", despite what we had been told in the past. This attitude was echoed at many levels of our society until very recently. Now, our society is beginning to realize that debt is not a good thing, not for the debtors, and perhaps not even for the creditors. When new attitudes towards debt develop, we can expect to see slower, but hopefully more sustainable growth in our institutions, but this will only occur after a possibly long and painful process of digging our way out of indebtedness. As President Walter Lingle of Davidson said, *"Perhaps it has been well that we have had to pause for a while as far as material things are concerned and place the main emphasis upon the things of the mind and spirit"* (6)

As the Great Depression began to lift, and the archival documents and records of charitable giving suggest that the psychology began to change after 1935, earlier than many today believe, the colleges realized that their survival was an accomplishment they could take pride in.

With the success thus achieved in keeping Lees-
McRae in operation and in continuing to make
progress in the improvement of plant and program in
the face of the depression, the 1936 commencement
exercise were in a considerable degree a celebration of
the permanency of the institution. (7)
Even through the depression years the enrollment has
steadily increased, and the quality of the students as
well as the number has been most gratifying. (8)

The federal and state governments became active partners in higher education through programs such as federal work-study, loans and grants to help finance college, and broader laws that encouraged charitable giving through tax incentives:

> The present income tax acts, both Federal and State, contain provisions as to the treatment of gifts made to educational and other charitable institutions. The acts permit a person making such a gift to deduct the amount of it from his taxable income up to 15% on Federal and 10% on the State of North Carolina.... (9)

Again, we see signs of increased federal and state activism to promote higher education as a long-term response to an economic contraction. Unfortunately, the years of global depression in the 1930's encouraged the growth of other social and political trends as well, as Davidson's President Walter Lingle describes in 1939:

> As these lines are written the world outlook is darker than it has been in the memory of this generation. Moral and spiritual ideals are being crushed in many and large parts of the world. Brute force and crass materialism are taking their place. Whole nations are now putting into actual practice what their leaders have been thinking and teaching for a good many years. We will never be able to overcome the forces of evil in the world by mere physical and intellectual development. Even Napoleon is quoted as having said: 'There are only two powers in the world, the spirit and the sword. In the long run, the sword will always be conquered by the spirit.'
> For ten or more years the nations have been feverishly re-arming. They are now reaping the results. The great need of the world today is for moral and spiritual re-armament. The only hope of the world lies in that direction. Christian colleges like Davidson are engaged in that great task. (10)

Hopefully, we can learn from history and avoid traveling the same path.

Today, some of these colleges have thrived and grown to institutions of national repute; some continue to struggle to meet yearly budgets, but all were profoundly shaped by their struggle through the Great Depression. These records provide us a glimpse into their struggles and triumphs. If there is one final lesson to be learned from these institutions, the survivors, it is that the will to survive seems critical. Some constituency - whether the local community, as with Louisburg College, the broad base of loyal alumni, as with Wake Forest, the almost familial ties between employees and administration, as seen in Campbell and Lees-McRae – refused to give up on the college and refused to despair. A weedy tenacity kept these places going eighty years ago; many of us will need that same tenacity and resolve today.

Citations

1. *Wake Forest College Alumni News* - April, 1931, Vol.3, No.5, *Increased Enrollment and How it Can Be Obtained.*
2. Louisburg College President's Report to the BOT, Armour David Wilcox, May 15, 1933.
3. Lees-McRae College, Edgar Tufts Memorial Association BOT minutes, October 20th, 1933.
4. Lees-McRae College, *Pinnacles,* January 1937, XXVI, *Education That Counts.*
5. Lees-McRae College, *Pinnacles,* January, 1934, XXII.
6. Davidson College President's Report to Board of Trustees, 15 February, 1933.
7. Lees-McRae College, *Pinnacles*, June, 1936, *Surviving the Depression.*
8. *Wake Forest College Alumni News,* May, 1937, Vol. 6, No. 4, *An Objective For 1937-38.*
9. Lees-McRae College, *Pinnacles*, December 1937, Vol. XXVI, *The Cost of Giving.*
10. *Davidson College Bulletin*, September 1939, *Are These Ideals Worth Striving For?*